FriesenPress

Suite 300 - 990 Fort St
Victoria, BC, V8V 3K2
Canada

www.friesenpress.com

ISBN
978-1-5255-0440-2 (Hardcover)
978-1-5255-0441-9 (Paperback)
978-1-5255-0442-6 (eBook)

1. BIOGRAPHY & AUTOBIOGRAPHY, PERSONAL MEMOIRS

Distributed to the trade by The Ingram Book Company

A Horror is just the Foreground to a Wonder
and we need not be Afraid of our Lives

PREFACE

I NEVER THOUGHT I WOULD WRITE AN AUTOBIOGRA-
phy, although I have always been enthralled by books and have
wanted to express myself through writing for as long as I can
remember. As a child, I was an avid reader and would voraciously
devour whole series of books: The Hardy Boys, Nancy Drew.
. .anything I could get my hands on through our limited school
library, or borrow from friends. All books were, and still are,
interesting to me. Even if they were too advanced, I would still
struggle to get the meaning of the difficult passages, and would
enjoy looking up and learning new words from the dictionary. I
remembered dialogues and complicated vocabulary, and used to
recite them as we were walking home from school, to the amuse-
ment of my sister and our friends. Sometimes I would be lying in
bed, half dreaming, and dialogues or conversations would come to
mind. If only I would have had the guidance and encouragement
to write them down, but of course such pursuits were "nonsense,"
at least according to my parents.

Mediocrity was encouraged over creativity; how interesting that
the tragic events of my youth would elevate me beyond that level
to success despite adversity, suffering, and sorrow, and that my
healing journey would lead me to view that shocking event as an

initiation into an uncommon life, lived to the fullest with creativity, purpose, and love.

The decision to tell my story came about during my healing process, at a point in my life when I finally had the time and energy to face my past. I had signed up for a storytelling workshop, and during an exercise to prepare the participants to share their past through myth, metaphor, and visual imagery, I had an epiphany. I *knew* that it was time to start writing, and I knew—with unerring certainty—what I was going to write about. It was time to heal my past by recording every detail of that painful and surreal time. Events and occurrences started to synchronize in my life to lead me to the culmination of this book. I met key people who were instrumental in validating my past, and assisted in my writing process. I returned to the Midwest for a family reunion and felt a connection to that land and those memories. This led me to move to an urban center not far from where I had grown up, and it was in that city that I started to write. Has this story ever been told by the perpetrator of the crime, exposed in all its painful clarity, profound sadness, and horror? I think not, and as to the fate and healing process of other mothers who have harmed their children at birth—although I sympathize and empathize with them—the trajectory of their lives is the subject of another book.

INTRODUCTION

WHAT YOU ARE ABOUT TO READ IS A TRUE STORY. IT IS about the tragedy of infanticide, and the story of one woman's lost and lonely childhood, abused and abandoned by a mother who in all probability had been abused herself. The tragedy still happens from time to time. One hears of a young mother who abandons her newborn in a public toilet, a garbage can, someone's doorstep, a hospital or church foyer. . .but things are different now. The mothers are encouraged to come forward for help and counseling; if the child survives, there are no charges laid. They have a chance to heal—hopefully to live in peace and have another chance at motherhood. But we never hear what happens to these women after the initial media frenzy, the public curiosity, the righteous judgment. Why did these women commit such a heinous crime? Do they go on to live productive lives? Do they become hopeless burdens on society, numbed by their pain, unable to survive without the crutch of prescription/street drugs or alcohol? Do some of them take their own lives, unable to live with the memories? What becomes of these mothers?

Many books on the subject have been written by professionals and academics, analyzing the societal and cultural symptoms, as well as the causes and effects of infanticide, but this may be the first book written by the perpetrator of the crime. In Meyer &

Oberson's *Mothers Who Kill Their Children: Understanding the Acts of Moms from Susan Smith to the "Prom Mom,"* they state, "There is a morbid curiosity in the United States relating to mothers killing their children."

A morbid curiosity and a difficult time struggling with how to place this crime. It is not a crime of passion, and people don't know what questions to ask to get to the core of it, so they remain silent. But their thoughts about it are disturbing. Mothers are ideally the nurturers and protectors of the young, not the destroyers, so who else but a monster would destroy an innocent, helpless infant? No one likes to think they have raised a criminal, so where does one place this crime, and how does one deal with it?

At the time I committed this crime, there were no counseling or support groups available, and little understanding of the need to address the underlying issues that led to it. How could I just go on living normally after what happened? Deal with the memories and flashbacks or talk about it? The listener is filled with horror and disbelief, the relater and perpetrator overcome with remorse and guilt, hoping for compassion and absolution, but often feeling blamed and condemned.

What you are about to read is the true story of a young girl who wasn't psychotic, insane, or mentally incompetent. It is an account of the life of an ordinary teenager who couldn't see any other way out; the life of a violated child who had learned to suffer abuse silently, who believed that there was no one to turn to, that everything was her fault, and that she could never tell a soul of the terrible thing she had done. . .but her secret was soon found out. Her community—indeed the entire nation—came to know about her mistake. It was exposed to the entire world, for she became a tragic statistic along with all the other young mothers who have destroyed their children at birth. From the memory of a terrified, emotionally alienated teenager who stared death in the face and survived. . .this is my story.

CHAPTER I

The Abandoning

"BE READY ANY TIME," SHE TOLD US IN A HUSHED VOICE one early spring evening. "Pack a small suitcase, hide it under the bed, and when I come and tell you, be ready to go, because we're going to leave your father."

We weren't given any other information, and didn't dare ask. I don't remember how long my sister and I had to live with that secret, or if we even dared discuss it between ourselves in private. It seems it was a week or two later that she came to us as we were getting ready for bed. "We're going tomorrow morning," she said. "Act normal and leave as usual, but don't go to school. Wait on the corner by the service station, and I'll meet you there with your brother. Don't say a word to anyone. We'll be taking the bus to the city." All this was spoken in hurried, hoarse whispers so as not to alert my father. My sister was 13, I was 11, and my brother was 4.

It was May, and the following morning dawned bright and sunny. As usual, in springtime in the Midwest, my father was leaving for a long day in the field. Never one to express emotion, how interesting that he kissed us children goodbye that morning before leaving, something he had never done before. Choking back the

1

tears, I felt I was betraying the one stable parent who, up until that time, I don't remember ever physically abusing me. It would be several weeks before we would see him again.

We boarded the bus under the watchful eye of the local barber, who later told my father that my mother had left with all three of us on a school day. Until we got our own apartment, we stayed with a friend of our mother's who she had met in our town, and who had since moved back to the city. This family had moved to our small town temporarily to work, and I had gone to school with the youngest daughter, who was my age. My father always blamed this woman for encouraging and helping our mother leave the farm. "If it weren't for that meddling bitch," he used to say, "your mother would have been here where she belonged."

My mother was physically, emotionally, and mentally abusive, and her abusive behavior became even more difficult to deal with once we were living with her in the city. The stress of trying to hold down a full-time job and raise three kids by herself was too much for her, and the abuse escalated. My older sister, always the leader in those days, accused her of being a hypocrite one day and suffered a harsh slap across the face for her honesty. We were expected to jump to her bidding and every command. She was quick-tempered and unstable, always ready to fly off the handle at the slightest vexation. She was determined to control her two beautiful, adolescent daughters—to make them heel.

"You'll respect me, I'm your mother!" she would shrill, knowing that her control was slipping even as she uttered the words. She was jealous of the youth, beauty and future of her two maturing teenagers and the responsibilities of single parenting were too overwhelming for any self-control—the reminder of her own lost youth and romance too vivid and apparent in the blossoming of her daughters.

We finished the last two months of school in the city that year, grade eight for my sister and grade seven for me. My beautiful sister, mature for her age, was starting to run with a too-wild crowd, and I was learning schoolyard vocabulary that I never knew existed. I missed my friends and my small-town baseball team; the June tournament that I had been looking forward to, and dreading at the same time, was just a distant memory now that we had moved to the city. I did enjoy meeting new friends and all the amenities urban life provides, to say nothing of the interesting characters that populate a city. I don't remember us ever asking about our father during that time, as we were always careful to avoid provoking any raging attacks from our mother, but I definitely did miss him.

We didn't get to see our father until late June. One day my mother announced that we were traveling to a neighboring city for a meeting with the two lawyers. At that meeting, we all burst into tears when we first saw our dad.

"It's obvious that the children love and miss their father," my dad's lawyer said. Usually so well-groomed when not working on the farm, I remember that he was unshaven and looked tired, stressed, and worried. The two lawyers, in their divine wisdom, decided to separate us three children; my sister and I were to live with our mother in the city, and our 4-year-old brother was to live with our father in the country. They drew up a separation agreement, which included my sister and me spending the month of July with our father and brother on the farm. My father left that day with our brother, and it felt strange to be without him in the city. He was little more than a baby, and really must have missed his mother, as she doted on him.

We were looking forward to going back to our life on the farm and to seeing all our friends. I wondered how much everyone knew, the scandal of it all, as no other mother had ever just up and left like that. I don't remember anyone else's marriage breaking up in all the years I went to school there; if there were problems, women just stayed and coped somehow—had affairs, took up new hobbies, redecorated the house, had nervous breakdowns, or once in a while even blew their brains out—but no one had ever just taken the kids and left.

The following month we went to visit our father for summer holidays, as per the separation agreement, and we were happy to be back in familiar surroundings, spending time with our friends. About halfway through our visit, my sister brought up the idea of us staying permanently to live with our father and brother. We began to discuss how we didn't want to go back to the hell of life in the city with our mother, and I definitely wasn't going to return without my sister. I remember the day we told our father. It was a Sunday and we had just returned from a tour of the farm "to have a look at the crops." It was something our father liked to do occasionally: take a drive with us kids through his crops, proudly explaining which grain it was, and what yield he expected it to produce. I wasn't much interested in these excursions at the time, as I found them boring and we had to endure fat grasshoppers jumping in and out of the open car windows, but I realize now that he was proud of his work on the land, and it was his way of assuring us that he could provide for us.

We were still sitting in the car after our trip to the fields. It was hot and the wind rustling through the caragana bushes lining the driveway provided a lovely breeze into the opened car windows.

"We're not going back," my sister said. "We want to stay here with you and go back to our old school."

He told us we didn't have to go back if we didn't want to; he assured us that this was our home and he wanted us to stay so that we could all be together. He was happy to have us back, and so the fight was on. He was contravening a judicial order, and now there would have to be a court case to let a judge decide.

I remember well the day he took us back to the city to get our clothes and to tell our mother that we wouldn't be back to live with her. She was expecting our return at the end of July to prepare for the upcoming school year, as it was the end of our month-long holiday in the country. He didn't have the backbone to go in and tell her himself, nor had he prepared her with a phone call or letter to let her know the change of plan. No, he sent my sister and me, at 13 and 11 years old, to take care of an adult responsibility. Better that we should face her wrath at being permanently separated from her children, than our father: a strapping macho man who regularly lifted weights.

We approached the house and I had a sick feeling in my stomach, knowing exactly what kind of reaction awaited us. It was a white, colonial-style building on a corner lot, one of those lovely, older homes that had been remodeled and converted into separate suites. Our apartment was on the main floor; I remember it had spacious rooms, high ceilings and big bay windows that looked out onto a treed yard and main avenue.

We entered the house, and upon hearing the news that we would be returning to the country to live with our father, she started screaming and howling like a banshee. Barring the door and pre-venting us from going into our bedroom to collect our things, she terrified us by pulling and clutching at our clothes, hysterically raging that we couldn't leave, and running after us—yelling and screaming hysterically—as we fled to the safety of the waiting car. The other tenants of the house, and people on the street, stopped to stare. She was screaming to see our brother, who was sitting waiting in the car with our father. As my sister and I ran in terror toward the vehicle, my father started the car and told us to just get in. We jumped in and my father took off, with my mother shrieking and out of control, grabbing at the moving vehicle. Now she knew her fate: she had her freedom, but she would go it alone. . .without her children.

"Never mind about your clothes," my father said. "We can go shopping for more." He took us to the summer fair that day, which helped to ease some of the pain of that horrible experience.

We started back to school in the country that September, and life was more or less back to normal at home, except that now my sister and I had to do all the housework and then some. But more about that later. At least there was relative peace and quiet, with no more histrionics or witnessing my parents fighting—a terrifying memory for me as a child. Sometime later, our father told us we would be traveling to the city in November to attend the custody hearing. Everyone knew that this was the day of reckoning, as we had to miss school and none of us knew if my sister and I would be returning. Quiet and subdued, the four of us drove to the city that cold November day, no one knowing if we would be coming back home to our country life or living in hell in the city.

The three of us sat in the courtroom along with the other adults, including my father's character witnesses from our town—pillars of the community who had known him since he was a boy, homesteaders who had founded the community along with our paternal grandparents. The presiding judge noted that the ensuing testimony wouldn't be appropriate for us children, so the three of us were soon ushered out. We were taken to a large room with lots of windows, filled with a large, rectangular mahogany conference table, where we remained while the judge decided our fate. Individually the three of us children had been interviewed by the judge prior to the trial. "Who does the dishes and makes the beds?" he asked me. "Who gives your little brother his bath?" A man of about fifty with dark hair and glasses, he was kind and seemed genuinely concerned about our well-being.

After about three hours of waiting, the verdict was in and it was decided that the three of us were to live with our father in the country. Our father had won custody of his three children! The judge had labeled our mother unstable, my father told us later. This judicial order was highly unusual in rural America in the sixties; mothers almost always got custody of their children in those days, unless there was evidence of alcohol or drug addiction, which wasn't the case with our mother.

I remember her bursting into the room after the court case. "I hope you're happy now," she hissed in my sister's face, and grabbing our brother, announced that she was taking him out to lunch. My father hesitated.

"Just let him go," his lawyer said. "She knows she has to bring him back." The rest of us went out for lunch as well: my father, his lawyer, and my sister and I. We were all relieved and happy that it was over, and that we were going back home for good.

Some years later, our father told us that one of our neighbors had said to him, "Don't worry; the girls will be back." I'm sure that many of the townspeople expected and wanted us back and were glad that we had returned home.

There were specific court-ordered monthly trips to the city to visit her, as well as three days at Christmas and Easter and a month during the summer holidays, all at my father's expense. These were mandatory visits until we reached the age of 16, at which time we could choose to go or not. We accepted our fate, but could hardly wait for that birthday, when we stopped the visits, although by then I had developed many friendships in the city and I did miss them, as well as the ambiance and variety of city living. To this day, I prefer city life to the country. . .one reason being its anonymity.

CHAPTER 2

The Pedophile

"YOUR MOTHER WENT HAYWIRE," MY FATHER USED TO say, "after she found out about her father." My grandfather had raped and impregnated a 14-year-old foster child—my mother's best friend—in their home. The child, who was the same age as my mother, had been placed in my grandparent's home when she was 9. My sister and I were small children when our mother found this out, and she told us the truth when we were old enough to understand. I can't remember a time I didn't know about my grandfather, the rapist. One day her friend simply disappeared, my mother told us, and she and her younger sister, my aunt, were told that Child Protection Services had taken her back. No further explanation was given or required, as children never questioned their parents' dictates in those days, but my mother always wondered what had become of her close childhood friend. Nothing more was said about her, and years later, after my mother had married, moved to the Midwest, and had us two girls, she decided to try and find her long-lost companion.

She contacted Childhood Protection Services in the East, who passed her letter on to her friend, who at that time was living in New York. The two girlhood friends connected, started communicating, and the terrible truth came out. Despite this new-found awareness of her father, my grandfather, the pedophile, could do no wrong in my mother's eyes. He was always "Daddy" to her, and in her opinion, it was my grandmother's fault that he had repeatedly raped an innocent child. According to my mother, my grandmother was the "cold bitch" who had denied him sex, "forcing" him to turn to a mere child who didn't know the difference between sex and affection. That determined child had left my grandparents' home, fought to keep her baby, and won, which in those days was very difficult, as back then there weren't the choices and social services available to the single mothers of today.

My sister and I grew up knowing about our "aunt" and her family of five children, all of them successful in the entertainment and modeling business. "I was an innocent child," she told me years later, when I finally met her during a visit to New York in my twenties. "I didn't know anything about sex or where babies came from. I just thought your grandfather was being affectionate with me. I had no idea what had happened until one day he noticed that my skirts were getting tight, and asked me when last I'd had my period."

She always spoke openly about her past, never hiding the truth from her husband or any of her children—not even from her first child, the child she had struggled to keep and raise on her own and who later became a very successful professional.

There is a picture of the two of them, my grandfather and my mother, the one time my grandparents came out West to visit us. He is seated, with his pipe in his mouth, while she stands behind him, her hand lovingly on his shoulder with a look of nostalgia and sadness on her face. My sister and I were around 3 or 4 that first time we met him, the pedophile, accustomed to his male entitlement. There are pictures of my sister and me, playing with him, he on all fours with the customary pipe in his mouth, and my sister and I riding "horsey" on his back. I don't remember any of that visit, but it was around that time that my sister and I started to masturbate each other in the outhouse. This was something we did in secret and often, soon to be discovered by our mother. Not unkindly, she forbade us from doing that, explaining that it wasn't acceptable behavior, and we stopped.

The year before my mother disappeared from the farm with us, she had taken the three of us kids to visit her parents in her hometown: a large city in the East. We spent the summer there in the suburbs. My mother worked as an office temp downtown, and we spent most of the summer sitting in the humidity under a weeping willow tree in their small corner lot. We had taken the cross-country train to get to the city; it was my first trip so far away from home, and it was exciting for me to travel through the different geographical landscapes, watching the scenery chug by, and meeting the various characters that got on and off throughout the long journey.

Unfortunately that was the best part of the trip. Our grandparents met us at the railway station downtown, and at that moment on the busy street, our big brown suitcase flew open. I remember a sea of white clothing strewn over the pavement, my mother's predictable hysterics, and the huge skyscrapers looming over my head. The brisk wind from the lake whipped my hair about my face as I stared up at those enormous buildings—the first I'd ever seen. Our grandparents were truculent at best, and years later, my grandmother told me that that summer our mother had wanted to leave our father and stay and work in the city. She had asked her parents to look after us kids. They declined, saying that they were too old, and that she should return with us to our father, as they had always liked him and they believed that was the best place to raise us kids. I remember the pedophile squeezing my hips that summer and laughing heartily through the clenched pipe between his teeth. I can only imagine what my sister and I would have endured had our grandparents agreed to our mother's plan.

To this day, my mother still speaks lovingly of her father; she never mentions her mother. She always honors "Daddy's" birthday and the anniversary of his death, talking about him and reminiscing. Whenever I think of him, I want to throw up.

One thing is certain: my grandparents never knew that my mother had contacted her childhood friend, nor that they had visited back and forth. My grandmother especially would have been outraged at my mother's audacity.

CHAPTER 3

My Early Childhood

AN INTERESTING INCIDENT COMES TO MIND WHEN I think of myself as a very young child. I was standing in front of a metal trailer with my parents, and I think, my sister. My father used the trailer to haul wheat, and it was parked at the edge of our property, which faced an open field that ended at the east/west-running highway about a mile away. All of a sudden, a bullet whizzed by my nose and embedded itself in the metal trailer, just a few inches from my face. A hunter perhaps, shooting gophers or rabbits from the distant highway? That was an unusual experience and my first brush with death.

My earliest memories are of my parents fighting, constantly and viciously. There was always tension in the home, and I can remember my sister and I cowering in fear in the stairwell while the fights raged on. Sometimes we would be ordered upstairs or outside; often we were ignored in the heat of the moment. I remember feeling that it was my fault that they fought. I hadn't been good. . .you know how children blame themselves.

My parents would fight about the house and farm duties, about money, and about us children—what we could or couldn't do, or should or shouldn't eat. He would beat her, and she would call him every filthy name under the sun, her sexual frustration given a voice, "Good-for-nothing, scum-of-the-earth bastard!" They would also throw things at each other. The wallpaper in that old house—with its pattern of poodles at an outdoor café, in yellows and pinks—still had the streaks of liquid down its length years later, where my father had thrown a cup of something at her.

Having gone to the city to select a farm wife, my father had unrealistic expectations of his new young bride who was twelve years his junior. She was expected to adjust to the rigors of farm life in the fifties; she was supposed to just know what to do and do it uncomplainingly, coming from the amenities of living in the city to a two-room shack with no running water or indoor plumbing.

Maybe there would have been a chance for that adjustment if he had paid some attention to her, for she was still a 19-year-old teenager with stars in her eyes, and she wanted a romance with her prince charming. No way. Not for him. His thinking was, "It's time to get down to business and build a farm and raise a family. There's plenty of work to be done. The honeymoon's over."

She was too immature and determined to have her own way to make any compromises for a successful marriage. Years later, when I was in my twenties, I visited my grandmother and she told me how she had cautioned my mother about the farm life that awaited her. Talking woman to woman, she asked me, "If your father wanted a farm wife, why did he come to the city and marry a young girl?" She told me that she had explained to my mother how difficult it would be to adjust to that life, so many miles away from her familiar surroundings and city lifestyle. My mother had responded with the predictable answer of all inexperienced young women in love: She would follow my father anywhere and together they would work it out and be happy—the innocence and illusion that love would conquer all.

My mother was too emotionally unstable and finicky to adjust to prairie life; she was never able to handle the duties of farm wife and mother even under the gentle guidance of my paternal grandmother. She refused to collect the eggs from the hen house, nor would she wash the cream separators from the cows. My father had hopes of maintaining a self-sufficient farm like the one belonging to his sister, my Aunt Nelly, with chickens, cows, and maybe even pigs and horses. But he was unable to do it all without her help, so he resigned himself to being a grain farmer. When I was about 8 or 9, my father invested in turkeys. There were lots of them, well over a thousand. I remember they used to wake us up at five in the morning with their gobbling. That only lasted a couple years, then he went back to wheat farming.

The worst part of the fighting was that they took it out on us. She had my sister and me so tyrannized that we would jump at the sound of her raised voice. She would follow her vitriolic diatribes with beatings. She was never mature enough to accept her life and her responsibility as a parent, nor was she able to control her rage. She would fly off the handle at the slightest provocation and demanded that we completely obey her every order. If we didn't snap to attention fast enough at her demands, she'd yell, "Do as you're told or I'll crack you across the face." But her preferred abuse was hair-pulling, followed by hysterical, tearful declarations of how sorry she was and how much she loved us.

When my sister and I were teenagers, after my mother had already left, one of the farm women told us, "Your parents were *so* in love when they were first married." There are pictures of them holding us as babies. . .intimate, close, and laughing. Many years later, after my father's death, one of the women from the town, who was a teenager when our parents were first married, wrote us a letter:

"Thank you for the pictures of the farm where you can see Gramps' farm in the distance. I remember walking to your dad's farm to see the new baby (my older sister). *Your parents made quite an impression, your mother with her laugh and your dad with his big cigar, talking and laughing with the men..."*

After my father's funeral, I read and reread that letter so many times, as it gave me a glimpse of how it must have been between them in the early days—something we kids rarely witnessed. I can only remember one occasion when my parents were acting lovingly toward each other. She was sitting on his knee as he sat in his favorite chair in the kitchen, between the table and the fridge. She was laughing and happy; he was smiling.

But the dream quickly soured, and she constantly vented her rage and pent-up frustration on her children. I remember one terrifying incident when I was about 5 or 6. I was drying dishes standing beside her at the kitchen counter while she kneaded bread. I dropped a Melmac plastic cup and the sudden noise so incensed her that she flew into a rage and started screaming at me and pulling my hair with her dough-covered hands. I had disturbed her self-indulgent reverie, and she spewed her rage on me. I thought she was going to kill me. I was severely traumatized and felt so unworthy and unloved. But this incident taught me volumes. I knew that I could never trust her with my true feelings, and especially that I had to hide any negative emotions I was feeling. So much violence, and so many negative experiences as a young girl also taught me that I had no right to be treated with respect, that I had no voice, and had no say in whatever happened to me. I knew I couldn't tell her about any problems I was having, because it might upset her more, so I learned to hide everything inside and try to figure it out myself. Just put on a smile and hide the pain. It took me a long time to get the wet dough out of my hair, and to this day, I don't like anyone touching or playing with my hair too much; it still brings back unpleasant memories.

My father's brand of abuse was that he wasn't at all affectionate. Mostly he would ignore us, and when he did pay attention to us, he would play with us roughly. A favorite game of his was to "play prisoner." He would hold my sister and I trapped between his crossed ankles, and we would struggle and scream for help to get out. He would also displace his rage at our mother and direct it at us for an innocent question. Once he asked me to go downstairs to get a couple of eggs. I asked him how many a "couple" was, and he glared at me as if he wanted to kill me. His eyes were terrible. "Are you stupid or something? Don't you know how many a couple is?"

He was a big man and having that hateful energy directed at me, a small child, was terrifying. Later on, when my sister and I were developing teenagers, he would touch us inappropriately. I don't mean groping our private parts, or openly touching us sexually, but he would run his fingers lightly down our arms and say some nonsense words with a ridiculous exaggerated expression on his face. It used to make my skin crawl. We had to pass him in the morning on the way to the porch, where we would wash up at the sink, and he would usually start the day with this routine, putting me in a bad mood, which he then berated me for, saying I was a "bad-tempered bitch" and that I shouldn't be bothered by his touching, because someday I would be married and would have to get used to a man touching me.

This displacement of sexual energy toward children is called covert sexual abuse, and it is just as damaging as overt sexual abuse, if not more so. It is easy for the perpetrator to deny any offense, as outwardly it looks harmless, and the repulsion and discomfort of the victim can be easily dismissed by the perpetrator as the victim "not being able to take a joke," being "uptight or bad-tempered," or simply "imagining it." That was definitely how I was treated. This type of abuse causes deep mistrust and aversion to males in developing adolescent girls, as well as a warped sense of values. He would also tell off-color, inappropriate jokes, and then laugh uproariously at our discomfort. "If I were a younger man, I'd be considered virile," he used to say. Or he would seek solace and confirmation in being "the good parent" by complaining about our mother and reminding us of all the mean things she used to do, and how she had said terrible things about him.

This parentification, or role reversal of the child, robs children of their innocence and childhood, projecting the responsibility to understand and judge the other parent onto an inexperienced mind, creating doubts and uncertainties. Obviously his sexual compass was completely off; he never had a girlfriend after my mother left, but every once in a while, he would take an overnight trip to the city, cautioning us to lock the door at night, and not to open it to strangers.

Our mother also displayed inappropriate sexual energy toward my sister and me. "What have you got on?" she would say, and lift up our dresses and skirts with a big swoop of her arm, exposing our underwear, all the while laughing gleefully. Another time, I remember she made me wash her genitals as she was lying in bed, as she claimed she was too sick to do it. "What do you think nurses have to do in hospitals?" she shrieked, the strong genital odor wafting up and prickling my nostrils, as I did my best to clean her without demonstrating my revulsion. Later on, after she was separated from our father, she told me that my father had "latent homosexual tendencies," and added, "Your father had a nice penis, but he never wanted to use it."

What is a 14-year-old supposed to say to those kinds of comments?

One very sad, tragic memory I have of my childhood was when my sister and I threw sand in a baby's eyes. Some people were visiting on a Sunday afternoon. I don't remember them as being close friends and I don't think they lived in our town. The adults were in the house chatting, and the baby was sleeping in the carriage, in the shade by the side of the house. The child woke up screaming, and we were scolded severely. Why would two young children do something like that? Maybe because violence was all they knew and they were jealous of the love and attention being lavished on the baby; loving care and attention was something they never received in their world of fear and abuse. Years later, my mother, who was never able to take responsibility for her dismal failure as a mother, said, "Oh, it's a good thing you didn't get into real trouble for that."

Already a parent with grown children, I remember thinking what a pathetic excuse for a mother she was. Decades later, she still couldn't face the truth of her failure to guide and nurture her own children. I have never respected her nor will I ever be close to her. She has lived her life in denial; it was always someone else's fault, never hers, and she has paid a very high price for that attitude: physically, mentally, and emotionally. I have become a success in my life in spite of her, not because of her, and all the accolades I've received as a parent are from my determination and learning how *not* to parent as she did.

As a child I remember being so embarrassed by my beautiful, exotic mother. She didn't look like the other girls' mothers, nor did she dress like the other farm wives. She used to order her clothes from a special mail-order catalogue, which she also sold for a time. The designs would come in a thick book—page after page of illustrations of all the different styles, with colored swatches of material at the bottom. I used to love to look through that design book, feel the textured cloth samples, and imagine myself wearing fashionable fun clothes as a grown-up. Around that time she also had a mail-order bra business and I remember the ladies coming over to try on bras that promised to increase their bust; there was laughter and good fun as they tried on the different styles.

Our mother would get *so* dressed up, much more than the other people in our small town, and they always used to stare at her and gossip about her. I just wanted to crawl away and hide. She used to sell Avon along with the fashion wear, and would get dressed to the nines to visit the ladies with the catalogues, teetering on her high heels down the rough country roads. I can remember people asking me a lot of questions after she left: "Why did she dress like that?" and "Where was she from?"

Our mother had nothing but scorn for women who didn't dress ostentatiously, and would often criticize the farm women for their "dowdy" fashion sense, describing one local teacher as, "dressed in a gunny sack, waving a degree."

When my sister and I were about 8 or 9, she decided that we should have new outfits for fall, so *she* picked them out of the Sears catalogue. It didn't matter that I didn't like the bright red knee-high stockings with multicolored garter on top, or that I felt conspicuous and out of place walking into the church late—she was always late everywhere she went—or that everyone was staring, giggling, and pointing.

She used to love to dress up in jewelry and fancy dresses with bold patterns and colors, her dark, curly hair adorned with flowers, and she used to love to dance, which she continued to enjoy into her 80s. She was petite and shapely, and had a fun, infectious, raucous laugh, which made everyone exclaim, "Oh your mom is so much fun, so vivacious, and has such a nice personality!" How little they knew of her vicious, mean, Jekyll and Hyde personality, a multi-split disposition that vacillated between piggish, selfish, mean, and abusive behavior, to a slutty wanton image. And then there were the refined tones and manners she liked to teach her daughters.

She would often use this "teaching of manners" to shame us. When we were about 14 or 15, during one of our duty visits to her in the city, we were invited to a bridal shower at an acquaintance's home. All the guests, including my sister and me, were seated on chairs set up around the living room, and as the house filled up with people, she tried to make us sit on the floor, snapping her fingers and glaring at us to do her bidding, not daring to yell at us and embarrass herself in front of so many people. We refused to obey her and paid the price later, but it was worth it to challenge her authority and win.

I have few memories of my mother being kind or supportive to me, particularly in stressful situations, but I do recall one incident. I had always taken an interest in cooking and baking, and I had proudly followed a recipe and baked a cake. I think I was around 7 or 8. In my excitement at taking it out of the oven, I dropped the whole thing upside down on the floor. Fully expecting to get my hair ripped out of my head or to be slapped, for once she had compassion for my tears and said, "Don't worry; we'll just say it's pudding, serve it with a sauce, and no one will know the difference." So we salvaged what we could from the floor and did just that.

She had always been proud of our scholastic ability, and I remember feeling supported about that. "Just do your best," she'd say in her better moments. "You can't do better than your best."

She also taught us the importance of good hygiene. Without running water, as was the situation in many farm homes in those days, we had a stand-up sponge bath every day and a bath once in a while. As we neared puberty, she taught us to clean our vaginas every day and change our underwear, to use deodorants and creams, and the importance of being clean and sweet-smelling. Not like some of the farm girls who stunk so badly, that you could always tell when they had their period. I remember once when I was working in the library, I almost fainted from the fetid swamp-like odor wafting down from the skirts of a chubby classmate, as I held the ladder steady for her while she placed books on the top shelf. Basic hygiene may seem like a given nowadays, when everyone takes a shower before leaving the house, but in those days, there were still many farm homes without indoor plumbing, and it was obvious that many students didn't bother to wash or change their clothes regularly.

A couple years later, when I was in grade nine, our French teacher called all the girls in the high school into one of the classrooms, and looking very embarrassed, with her mouth pursed primly and eyes fluttering heavenward (she always did that when she was nervous), she told us that a male bus driver had complained to her about the way some of the girls smelled at certain times of the month. It was offensive to everyone riding the bus, and we should all make an effort to improve our hygiene.

Mostly we didn't go out as a family when my mother still lived on the farm, as there was so much stress generated by her constant histrionics. We went on one vacation while I was in elementary school. I remember it was a canyon resort where we rented a cabin for a week and swam in the pool every day. Many families had a cabin where they went every summer, but we just went that once. When we were a little older, we went to a church camp in the summer and our mother came along as a camp counselor. That was a horror show, with her competing for all the attention, and as usual, embarrassing us in front of the other kids.

Another time we took a weekend trip to a nearby city and stayed at a motel. I remember our room was on the second floor and there were two double beds and a TV. That was a real luxury for us, as TVs were just becoming popular in the fifties, but we never had one. My father always refused to get one, even years later, and he used to say that he wouldn't buy one until he was too old to do anything else but sit around all day. He was as good as his word. I noticed that he always enjoyed watching other people's TVs; he just didn't want to spend the money to buy one for himself. Eventually he inherited my grandmother's when she passed away some twenty years later.

During that motel visit, my mother was nagging and ranting at my father for something and he was ignoring her, just watching TV impassively. She worked herself into such a rage and frustration at his silence that she finally threw a telephone book at him, hitting him in the stomach. He turned white, got up off the bed, and slapped her hard several times. My sister and I were terrified and cowering on the bed.

There were other excursions which made me glad we could hide out at home. The first was a chance to look at the flax crop very early one June morning. In the springtime, the flax crops have beautiful blue flowers that bloom only once in the early morning light, then the petals close; if you arrive too late, you've missed it. This is a very beautiful sight, when you can see a whole field of blue blossoms in the golden light of dawn, or several fields, interspersed with the black, furrowed strips of summer fallow. We were excited about seeing the spectacle, but the early morning preparations for leave-taking squelched the joyful anticipation—with my mother screaming at us and slapping us when we protested sleepily at getting up so early, and yelling at my father to hurry up. What a nightmare. Thank heaven there was no one else around to witness it.

The second outing was a most unpleasant evening when we went to a movie in a neighboring town. Afterwards we were sitting in the local café, having refreshments. My father had neglected to take off his hat and this displeased my mother, who was particular about manners in other people, but was a master at being rude and ignorant herself. She began to natter at him to take off his hat in a constant monologue, her voice getting louder and louder. My father, not wanting to make a scene in public and looking more and more uncomfortable, remained silent, yet he stood his ground, and refused to obey her orders and take off his hat. I found the courage to protest and say something; I either told her to hush or to leave him alone. I don't remember exactly what I said. She gave me a furious, "how dare you open your mouth" look, and although she did calm her diatribe, I paid the price. I was sitting beside her, and she started to pinch my leg under the table, pinching and pinching my thigh ever harder until we left the restaurant. I didn't make a move during this abuse; I just endured it in silence, because I knew I'd get it worse if I let on what was happening. When I undressed for bed that night, there was a huge purple bruise on my leg that took a long time to disappear.

My sister and I never dared say anything that would have upset her. We never complained, always keeping any hurts and disappointments to ourselves, to protect ourselves from her terrifying rages and the physical abuse.

I remember one time we went into the city with my mother and a friend of my father's. I don't know why our father didn't accompany us. I remember we left very early in the morning when it was still dark, with my mother driving and the friend on the passenger's side. He slid way over close beside her, with his arm around her shoulders, and my sister and I were sitting in silence in the back seat. I was wearing new pedal pushers, as they were called back then—now known as capri pants. As we walked around the city that day, the inside seam was rubbing against the inside of my thighs, making them raw, red, and chapped. It was very painful to walk, but I didn't say anything for fear of being slapped or yelled at. That was a very unpleasant day, and my thighs took days to heal. I was learning to endure pain in silence.

Without a TV for entertainment, long winter evenings were often spent reading, playing cards or board games. We used to play cribbage with our father and Scrabble with our mother. Even at this she was impatient and intolerant, bellowing, "I've got a word!" when she'd just finished playing, barely giving us a chance to think and make a play as beginners with a limited vocabulary.

"I never had finicky kids," she said years later. Of course she didn't; we were too tyrannized and abused to dare speak up and express our true feelings. We learned to hide them all for survival.

As children we would often go to my Aunt Nellie's for the weekend. She was my dad's older sister, and they had a complete farm with chickens, pigs, cows, dogs, cats, and a horse. I used to love going there because of the love, attention, and regular meals we had. Aunt Nellie would encourage my mother to sleep late in the back bedroom, and we would run out to the kitchen to be with our older cousins. My aunt had one of those huge farm kitchens with a big table in the middle, and everyone gathered around that table to chat and joke, discuss politics and any other interesting topic of the times. The adults would make a fuss over us, and our older cousins would tease us and play games with us. It was a happy, busy, productive environment, so different from the tension and chaos of home.

My aunt was a former schoolteacher, and she used to like to read the Playboy magazines my cousin's husband would leave behind, saying that they had "such good articles." We all teased her about that and she took the ribbing with good humor. You could talk about anything with my aunt. She was open-minded, always had an intelligent point of view, and liked to debate issues, as did my father.

Years later, my Aunt Nellie expressed how it used to bother her when she was witness to our mother's abuse and mistreatment of us—how we would jump whenever she spoke. Not bothered enough to speak up and do anything about it, of course, because back then, what people did in their own homes was nobody else's business. "I'm surprised she didn't put you out on the street once you moved to the city," she said, when I was in my twenties. Indeed, had we been forced to live in the city with her, I'm sure we would have ended up there.

Staying at home saved us the embarrassment of my mother's public displays, but it was no sanctuary. It was always a mess: papers, dirty dishes, piles of dirty laundry, and confusion everywhere. She seemed to resent doing any housework or cooking, and we would often come home after school to find dirty breakfast dishes still on the table, she in her housecoat, and the place a total mess, while she looked at pretty dresses in the catalogue. Or she would be out selling her mail-order merchandise. Hungry after school, we would come home and fill up on bread and jam, already accustomed to eating whatever happened to be there—no regular meals now a given. To this day, I still struggle with a life-long habit of overeating carbs.

"Is your wife sick?" a neighbor once asked my dad when he dropped by during the day, looking for our father. "She came to the door in her housecoat at around noon."

The school nurse came by a few times in those years and things were better when she dropped in. There was laughter and the house was cleaner and tidier. She was a heavyset, jolly woman in a navy nurse's uniform who would try to humor our mother into getting dressed and taking care of her children.

We did not have regular meals until after my mother had left the farm and my father cooked for us. In those early days, supper was often just whatever we could find after school in all the mess. I loved to go to my girlfriend's house after school, and marveled at the orderly, clean house, her mom practicing piano when we came in, greeting us warmly, then making us a nutritious snack. It was like a dream world from a magazine compared to our house.

Although I didn't have a happy childhood, or even a childhood at all in the sense of a carefree innocence and security, playing outside with happy abandon, or the comforts and love of a nurturing home, I have a few nice memories. In addition to the weekends spent at my aunt's house, I remember spending time with my paternal grandmother. My grandmother was a very gentle and loving woman who would try to teach my mother a kinder style of parenting. "No, that's not the right way," she would say when our mother would be screeching and slapping us for something, and then she would quietly discipline us. My grandparents had retired on the West coast, and I always liked it when they came back to the farm for the harvest season. I felt safe and loved with my grandmother.

I remember pleasant late-summer evenings when the adults would light the coal oil lamps, all of us crowded into the old homestead kitchen. The adults, my father and my grandparents, would be speaking German, talking about us and laughing, offering us cookies and commenting, I'm sure, on our size and robust appetites, which they themselves had condoned and created.

Sometimes the wind would come up strong, whipping around the old farmhouse, bending the bushes and whistling through the tall deciduous trees. Grandma would panic. "We'll have to take the kids into the root cellar," she would say. "There's going to be a storm."

"Take it easy, Ma," our father would say, reassuring her. "It's not that serious; everything is all right." When we had those prairie thunderstorms, dramatic displays of thunder and lightning, we used to feel terrified when we were little kids. She would sit on the couch with us, and explain that the lightning rods on the roof would protect us from harm, and we should just relax and enjoy the wonders of nature. My sister and I felt safe and protected, sitting on either side of her, one arm around each of us as we watched the storm.

Occasionally she would take us for walks to pick rose hips or Saskatoon berries to make jelly or jam, which she would later store in the root cellar under the kitchen floor. I remember once in my early teens collecting a jar of jam from the root cellar, which she had canned in the early 1950s. She tasted it and declared it fit to eat after some twelve years. It was delicious on homemade whole-wheat toast that she prepared for us.

My grandparents had homesteaded on the prairies in the Midwest in the early 1900s, and were hard-working European middle-class people. When they returned mid-summer to help with the harvest, we would often go out to visit them at the old farmhouse, and sometimes my sister and I would stay overnight.

In the morning, Grandpa would make us German-style pancakes, thin and as big as a plate, served with homemade chokecherry syrup. Meanwhile, we would crawl into bed with Grandma under the down quilt and she would tell us the story of her life in "the good old days." How she used to work from morning till night, raising five children in a four-room shack, the very one we were in now, planting a huge garden, putting up all the food for winter, keeping endlessly busy from morning till night. As small children my sister and I used to beg her to tell us those stories over and over again, and she would always end with, "Yep, it was a hard life, and I'd do it all over again."

CHAPTER 4

My Adolescence

"IT'S NOT TOO LATE TO GET THE SEED OUT," SHE SPAT, her eyes terrifying black holes of hell. I was 14 years old and had come in late from an outing with a church youth group, during one of our duty visits to the city. My sister and I had permission to go to these activities, but this particular night I had ended up driving around in a car with the preacher's 18-year-old wayward son, who usually avoided church and just showed up to ogle the girls. The preacher and my mother had been talking on the phone, discussing the possibility of our whereabouts, so by the time I arrived at the apartment about an hour later, around 10 pm on a Saturday night, my mother had had sufficient time to build a tale full of paranoia and untruths in her hysterical mind.

I was shocked to the core at her words and body language. We had just been driving around; maybe he had kissed me a few times. I didn't know what to say to her accusation. I knew about sex, and that most teenagers experimented; I even knew a couple friends who "went all the way" with their boyfriends, but the idea that I would just have sexual intercourse with a casual acquaintance at only 14 was really shocking to me. I started stammering in my fear of her, said I hadn't done anything, and went into the bathroom.

That must have made me look guilty, because she followed me in and barred the door, demanding that I undress so that she could purge the semen from my vagina. I managed to convince her that I hadn't had sex and was relieved to finally be able to go to the bedroom to share my story with my sister, who was equally horrified at our mother's insanely inappropriate behavior.

She had always instilled in my sister and me, a fear of sexual abuse from men, yet acted promiscuous herself. When we had visited our grandparent's city in the East 3 years previously, more than once she had made us very aware of the dangers of men. One Sunday we were window shopping, and my sister and I were running and jumping ahead of our mother and brother. She called to us sharply to come to her side, claiming that a man walking nearby was looking at us lasciviously. On another occasion, we were walking home from the main street down a shaded avenue on an early summer evening. She saw a man walking a block and a half behind us. She told us to run all the way home, as the man was holding something in front of his pants. I could feel her fear, and my own heart was beating like a trip hammer as the four of us ran in the summer humidity to our grandparent's house, through leafy elm trees casting shadows. During that same trip, on an excursion to a neighboring city to visit a girlhood friend of hers, we ended up staying overnight. My sister and I were put in bunk beds in an adjoining room from the adults. I remember being in the top bunk when one of the men from the party came into the room. I could smell his stagnant alcohol breath as he looked at me lying there, and I remember the paralyzing fear I felt. Our mother, or maybe it was her friend, came into the room and ordered him out.

When we took the train home from that summer in the East, she would settle us kids to sleep in our bunks, then would go up to the darkened dome car. My sister and I followed her up there one night, and as we crouched down in the back of the car, we saw her giggling and fooling around with a man.

Maybe it was her own childhood coming back to haunt her. How much buried abuse was there from that "Daddy" she so revered? Years later, as an adult, I could see the classic signs of a sexual abuse victim. Totally in denial about relegating blame to the male abuser, in addition to constantly referring to my grandmother as "that cold bitch," she always placed the blame on the woman whenever she heard of an incest or sexual-abuse case, whether on TV, in newspapers, or through community gossip. Even if it was a clear-cut case, again the onus was on the victim. "She should just completely forget about it," she'd say. "Just pretend it never happened."

She had many suitors after she moved to the city. My sister and I used to call her boyfriends "johns," as every time we arrived in the city for our monthly weekend visit, she had a new boyfriend. "Just one at a time," she used to say, and years later we would speculate on how many men she had slept with, calculating at least one a month over decades. They were all kind of weird, marginal types who didn't look that well-educated or intelligent. Many had strange accents or smelled of garlic, and talked too much. She would meet these guys at dance halls, or else through newspaper ads. Sometimes they would persist even after she was finished with them; there was one who came to the door of the apartment and tried to force his way in, with her screaming and trying to hold the door shut, and my terrified 5-year-old brother attempting to bar the door to help her keep him out.

Once we were back on the farm living with our father, we only had to endure these disturbing and dramatic scenes once a month. I felt I could finally relax and not have to be subjected to her hysteria, vicious sharp tongue, and physical abuse. The constant yelling and fighting of my parents, which seemed to erupt at the slightest provocation, were now a thing of the past, but neither of them ever let my sister and I forget how terrible the other parent was.

From the beginning of their separation, both of our parents denigrated the other in front of us kids. After he was given full custody of his children, and we were in the routine of visiting her in the city in accordance with the judicial order, she made her position clear: "If you ever need help," she said, "don't come crying to me— go to your father. He wants to be the *Great Provider*." She always said that with a sarcastic drawn-out exaggerated voice, jealous that he had been awarded custody of their three children.

Our father would comment on her vicious behavior and verbal abuse, and remind us of how she always said mean things about him. He ridiculed her and called her names, but he did say one accurate thing about her: "You can't be nice to her; if you don't stand up to her, she'll just destroy you." Years later, admitting at least some awareness and culpability of why she had left, he said, "In a relationship, it's the little things that count, and it's important to show kindness and attention to the other person. Trouble is, by the time a person learns that, it's too late."

All this criticism was very unpleasant to listen to and always made me feel uncomfortable, as I didn't want to have to choose sides. Neither one of them knew how to parent, and as the host of a popular TV show once said, "When there is domestic violence in the home, the children always pick up the tab."

"He makes a good babysitter," she used to tell everyone, trying to justify why she didn't have custody of her kids. I'm sure she never dreamed that when she left that day with the three of us, she would be denied her children, and that she would have to make her way through life on her own. Years later she admitted, "For all that I went through, I would have been better off to stay with your father on the farm." Indeed, and she would have had money, because that's the way it is in farming. You start out with nothing, deeply in debt, you work hard, and the dividends come later.

My initial euphoria at being back on the farm slowly changed to despair and depression at my lot in life. Our old farmhouse had no amenities—no running water, no indoor plumbing, not even a TV. My sister and I were expected to do all the housework, bake bread and do the laundry on Saturdays, and "be a mother to your little brother." I remember feeling completely overwhelmed by this last request. How could I get good grades, do all the housework and be a mother besides, when I was only 11 years old? The idea of getting outside help for the housework was not an option for my father, for no one was to come into our house to help. No, this was our private life, and what went on in our house was nobody else's business, no one else's concern.

Life became very bare bones and full of drudgery, stripped of any fun, creativity, or culture my mother had attempted to introduce into our lives. When she lived on the farm, she tried to introduce us to a variety of pretty things, in an extreme sort of way. For a while it was mail-order houseplants, and when that phase passed, it was mail-order long-playing records—a great variety of jazz, blues, gospel, country, and classical. Then she joined a book club and we were introduced to all kinds of books. Those were my favorites and I particularly loved the "Book Trails" series which contained eight volumes of illustrated fairy tales and parables.

There were many other kinds of books, including cookbooks, which led to her baking phase. She started making loaf breads of all kinds, experimenting with an assortment of tea breads such as cranberry and herbs, which weren't very popular back then, and yeast breads such as "featherbed" dinner buns with a sugar cube soaked in orange juice stuck in the tops before baking. There were also cream puffs of many varieties, tomato-soup cakes, marble cakes, and birthday cakes with waxed-paper-covered coins throughout the batter. The fruitcakes, which she particularly loved, she would order from the Sears catalogue and hide in the alcove, where she would secretly gobble them on her own.

She tried to bring some excitement and diversion to farm life and introduce us to some refinement and gentility, but without working shoulder to shoulder with my father in the creation of it. For his part, I could see how he gradually drove her further off the deep end with his boring, unromantic attitude and tightfisted ways. She wanted to invest in an apartment in the city; he wanted to pay off the farm as quickly as possible. He was extremely conservative with money, whereas she was a risk-taker interested in lucrative investments for future gain.

She introduced us to music, and my sister and I both took piano lessons and participated in recitals and festivals. Once we entered the annual variety show at the local town hall with participants of all ages and talents. We played a piano duet on one piano, dressed in identical dresses with our hair done up in pigtails, and we placed third in the contest. We couldn't have been more than 9 or 10. After the show, some of the adult contestants congratulated us on our performance, and that was an especially rewarding moment for me. I excelled in piano and won first prize in more than one recital, of which I was very proud.

I was hoping to resume piano lessons after my return to the farm, despite everything else I had to do, but my hopes were dashed. "You don't want to take piano lessons anymore, do you?" my father asked, once she was gone. So we quit music, the piano was sold, and I came to miss the solace of closing the door, forgetting the world and just playing my cares away.

Throughout our childhood, we were forced to endure our mother's religious inconstancy. She had been raised as a High Anglican, but chose to send us to Sunday school in the Protestant church rather than the Catholic church, which dominated our village. When a new Evangelical group came to town a year before she deserted the farm, she had my sister and I baptized in the local river, with mud and bloodsuckers oozing through our toes. These forays into spirituality did little to improve her behavior, but rather served to augment her already peppery vocabulary when describing her fellow parishioners. Those lacking (according to her) in righteousness were, "hypocritical, vain-glorying bastards," and then we knew we would be changing religions again.

"You've got enough work to do around here," was our father's standard response when we wanted to go to a school function in the evening, such as a basketball game or some sports event. The same went for weekends; in addition to doing the laundry on an old wringer washer, washing the floors, and looking after our little brother, our father insisted we bake wholewheat bread, from grain he had ground fresh from his crop yield.

Thrust into the role of raising three children on his own, our father became too strict with my sister and me, denying us the simple pleasure of an innocent school outing, instead creating the opportunity for us to lie and sneak out. "We're just going to a friend's house," we'd say, then end up in the back of someone's car with other thrill-seeking, bored teenagers and a case of beer, cruising the back fields with everyone drinking, including the driver. The risks we took back then! We had no understanding of the dangers of drinking and driving; there was no MADD, no designated driver or awareness training. We knew we weren't supposed to drink and drive, but everybody did it anyway. There were many car accidents during those teenage years, and there were a few who didn't come out alive or who suffered permanent debilitating injuries.

The adults were no better with regard to drinking and driving. My father wasn't a drinker, but he would always welcome the locals in for a Christmas drink on Christmas Eve. This was the tradition, going from house to house, drinking and driving in winter conditions, all the while getting more inebriated, well into the night. My sister and I used to spend the evening in helpless giggles as we watched our neighbors getting drunker and the conversation sillier. We also got to drink ginger-ale and eat sweets, which was a real treat for us, as my father rarely allowed us to eat refined sugar.

My teenage years were filled with longing and sadness, yearning for a mother to talk to, someone I could communicate with and discuss my problems and my dreams for the future. How wonderful it would have been to have been able to talk to someone who would have understood me without flying into a rage at the first word she didn't like—someone who didn't constantly try to control my very breath. It was always the same rhetoric: "You'll respect me; I'm your mother!" "You're just a child; you don't understand anything." "You'll do as I say, and *now*."

Our visits to the city were particularly unpleasant in the summer, as we had to stay with her for a month. She took out her resentment and jealousy of an unfulfilled life on us, her two beautiful, budding daughters. Her perceived powerlessness as a mother translated into scorn, rejection, and put-downs. "You're fat slobs," she'd say to my sister and me. "You have the figure of a 50-year-old woman." Meanwhile she was feeding us from cans during our visits. She never cooked a meal for us, thank God, for who could stand such mixtures as sardine and rhubarb soup, tuna salad sandwiches with cornmeal mixed in, thin porridge and powdered skim milk? Besides the canned food, there was lots of boxed macaroni and cheese, and little fresh food except for apples and oranges. "You look like you've been eating cornstarch," my father used to say when he picked us up at the bus after a month of summer holidays living with her in the city.

Whenever we were eating with a group in a restaurant, she would instruct us ahead of time to order a half portion only, then without asking, help herself to our plates, "just for a taste," and gobble down half of it. If we protested, we got slapped, pinched, or otherwise punished later. She was such a pig and so mean-spirited in so many ways. We were always encouraged to eat something at home before going out to eat anywhere, so we wouldn't "embarrass" her by ordering too much, or eating with healthy appetites.

For her daughters she only had meanness and criticism; meanwhile she doted on our little brother, showering him with whatever treats he wanted. If we commented on this favoritism, she would repeat, "Why don't you ask your father? He wants to be the *Great Provider.*" She had other expressions that made her rejection of us clear: "Be your own Santa Claus, and if you need help, don't come crying to me." "If you want to get ahead in life, you have to work like a bastard and don't expect anything from anybody." Yet she would lavish her son with gifts. When we were in the city for our regular visits, she would take him out and buy him anything he wanted and give him anything he wanted to eat. I never resented him because of her actions, as he was so young when she left and I know he suffered some dark years later on, I'm sure as a result of being separated from her at such a tender age.

In between city visits, she would send him parcels of clothes, shoes and books to the farm, even a set of encyclopedias, all addressed only to him. She once sent him a typewriter with an instruction booklet, and when she learned that I was teaching myself how to type with it, she suddenly needed it back; it was for him, not for me, and she demanded that I return it. Jealous perhaps, that I would upstage her lifelong career as a junior secretary? No, my childhood experiences spurred me on to seek a much better life, and a higher academic career.

I received one box of clothing from her when I was 18. It contained over-sized, outdated clothing and used underwear.

Throughout the years she would say, "I had three beautiful healthy children." Yes she did, but as one family member noted years later, "She didn't deserve them and was never a mother to them."

Our father was a health food advocate long before it became popular in the 60s, and made sure we had regular wholesome meals, something that we had never had when she lived with us. Once he was the main cook, our meals were predictable, plain, and highly nutritious. We had lots of farm-raised beef bought from a local farmer every autumn to store in our huge freezer. We had chicken and turkey, lots of eggs and cheese, a fish and rice dish once a week, and halibut in season in the springtime. We had baked potatoes or brown rice, and basic vegetables like carrots, onions and cabbage salad. Fruit was a box of apples and oranges, and there were sometimes bananas or dried fruit. We had the same meals week after week, and my father insisted we eat only whole foods. He used to lecture us on the importance of taking responsibility for our own health. His motto: Eat food that spoils quickly, but eat it before it does.

When I wanted to experiment with recipes from my Home Economics cookbook, making fancy European yeast breads at Christmas, he refused to buy white sugar as he said it was junk food that caused the build-up of waste and disease in the body. He was right about that and I'm grateful that he provided those nutritious meals for us.

However, we were always encouraged to eat too much, and we could never skip a meal even if we weren't hungry. "I went to the trouble of making it, you'll goddamn well eat it," he used to say. "And if you want to quit eating and don't like it around here, you can go down the road like your mother." From the time we were little, we had always been encouraged to eat every last food item on our plates. I can remember as a young child being late for school in the afternoon, because I had to eat every single last red kidney bean on my plate.

Our friends were always welcome to stay for dinner, as our father always enjoyed having guests over and would always invite them in to share whatever we were having. He enjoyed engaging in political or religious discussions with everyone and had that rare ability to converse objectively and intelligently without taking others' opinions personally. He was the only person I knew who would invite the Jehovah's Witnesses into the house on a Sunday afternoon, offer them coffee and spend a few hours discussing the bible.

My father liked to smoke cigars on weekends and a favorite time for us was Sunday mornings when he would make us fluffy whole-wheat pancakes, then puff on his cigar and give us advice about life. Friends would often drop by to join these philosophical discussions, or sometimes our uncle, who farmed with our dad.

As teenagers, we didn't see a lot of our grandparents, as they were getting on in years and had retired to the West coast. When they did come to visit, our grandmother would always ask what we planned to do after high school, then give us advice. University was discouraged, unless we knew exactly what we wanted to do before we started; studying for the joy of learning was considered frivolous and a waste of time.

Grandma tended toward a fatalistic, long-suffering view of life, particularly regarding men and sex. "I was expecting one, had another child at my breast, and one hanging on my skirt," she used to say, "and when I went to the doctor to ask for birth control, he said, 'Well Madam, this is a big country and we need more people to populate it.'

"Then after working all day on the farm, taking care of the children, cooking, cleaning, and gardening," she continued, "your grandfather would come home from the field and want sex, but that's the way it is for women, and the children make it all worthwhile."

Her advice to her teenage granddaughters? "Why bother going to university and having a career? You're just going to end up getting married anyway and staying home and raising the kids."

That's what you think, I said to myself, but I never expressed my hopes and dreams for my life, as I didn't trust anyone enough to share them. As a teenager I didn't have a clear idea of what I wanted to be, but I did envision myself working in a city, in a creative job where I could earn good money. Little did I know that the events of the next few years would forever completely change me and the direction of my life.

I had always been a sturdy child, but started to slim down as I approached puberty, around the age of 11. When my mother left, all that changed and I started to gain weight. By grade nine I was heavy, about thirty pounds overweight, and even though in our mother's absence we finally had regular meals, the emotional trauma and loneliness kept me chained to my old habit of eating bread, butter, and jam after school—a habit that took me decades to overcome.

By the eighth grade, most of my girlfriends had started their menses, and I eagerly awaited my first period. It showed up a few days before my thirteenth birthday, and I was very excited about it and wanted to share my feelings with someone. I told my older sister, who couldn't have cared less about the news, but I remember feeling proud and happy because now I was a *woman*. Not like some of the other farm girls, who not only didn't know how to keep themselves clean during that time of the month, they didn't understand the significance of it either. Some didn't have a clue that it had anything to do with sex and babies. One girl was so shocked to find blood on her panties that she thought she was bleeding to death. Her mother had told her nothing. She was horrified and disgusted to learn of the sex act and the fact of how she had come into the world. And her parents were supposedly educated people, prominent members of the community. Shame on them and their ignorance.

Our mother had explained to us about sex from an early age, answering our simple questions truthfully, and when the time came, she told us about the sex act—how it was a beautiful act between two people in love.

My high school years were full of turbulence, inner change and emotional isolation. The unhealthy environment and tension of living in a home with constant fighting were gone, but we were left with too many responsibilities and too little support; we were expected to all of a sudden act like adults without the guidance of a mother. Our father was gone for most of the day, working long hours during the planting season, leaving us to come home after school to an empty, lonely house. We would console ourselves with overeating and reading his magazines, which were forbidden to us—magazines that depicted violence against women, with stories of crime, prostitution, shootings, and sometimes even the torture of women. I never thought anything of it at the time, but it was desensitizing me and filling my mind with images of abuse and violence between the sexes, rather than positive expressions of healthy relationships based on caring and love. He would also read Reader's Digest and a religious magazine called *The Plain*

Truth, although he never set foot inside a church unless it was for a wedding or a funeral.

My father used to tell us that our teenage years were "the best years of our lives." I remember thinking, *If this is the best, well that's just depressing.* In the absence of our attending any extra-curricular activities at school, as we "had enough work to do at home," there was little else to do outside the house, as there never seemed to be enough money to go around. We did get a meager allowance, which we practically had to beg for, and when Saturday came around and we asked for it, he'd say, "Don't worry, you'll get it," and then forget about it, making us ask over and over again. I always hated that about him, how we had to grovel for a pittance of money. We even had to fight for the basics. If we needed clothes, he would try to avoid the whole issue of spending by saying, "We'll buy some next time we go into the city." Then when we went to the city, he would say, "We'll order them from the catalogue when we get home." When we were finally able to get new clothes, he questioned everything we bought and just wanted to buy the cheapest items, even if they were ugly, cheap-looking, or not in fashion. Not like the other girls, whose parents would take them to the city every fall before school started and outfit them for the season. I used to long for a nice wardrobe and enjoyed looking through the Sears catalogue when it arrived. And we did order most of our clothes from there.

When I started Home Economics in grade nine, I found it was easier to get material than to buy the finished product, so I became a good sewer, using our old-fashioned Singer feather-weight machine, which I still have. I failed grade nine due to all the turmoil and change in my life, but I always did well in Home Economics, English, and French, as I could pass those subjects and get a decent mark without studying.

Like any other typical teenager, I had crushes on boys, but I didn't really date anybody in high school. I was always attracted to the "bad boys," and for a time hung around with a local hockey player who was 21 to my 13. Going out meant driving around in the back seats of cars and drinking beer. He used to say, "I'm gonna go to jail; you're jail bait," but we only got as far as necking. I came close to going further than that one night. My sister and her boyfriend were in the back seat and we were in the front, but thank God nothing more happened and he moved on to someone else more willing to put out. There were a few more crushes, but it was mostly going out in groups, drinking beer in the backs of cars, going to dances in groups, and wishing someone nice would ask me out on a proper date. I think the boys were afraid of my father. I remember one weekend evening, quite late, a car drove into our driveway and a young man shouted, "Hey, why don't you let us take out your daughters?"

I was hoping my father would let me date as I got a little older, but he wouldn't allow it: an attitude which encouraged more lying and duplicity. He wouldn't let us go out on dates or ride in cars, so we would sneak out and do it anyway. I remember once a local boy, whom my father knew quite well—in fact our families had always been good friends—called me up and invited me to a high school dance. I asked if I could go out with him. My father said no, so I went to the dance with a girlfriend and ended up in the back seat of a car drinking lemon gin with someone far less responsible. In retrospect, he was afraid for us, and had no idea how his decisions and the events of my childhood and adolescence would culminate in a tragedy that would bring heartache to us all.

CHAPTER 5

The Beginning of my Descent into Hell

I COULDN'T BELIEVE IT WHEN I FIRST MISSED MY PERIOD at 17. How could this be? It must be impossible. I was worried, overtired, the very idea must be a figment of my imagination. It was my first sexual experience—date rape they call it now—and he hadn't even broken my hymen.

The family was new to our town. The kids attended our high school and his sister was in my class. She was a nice enough girl, a bit naive and simple, but we got along. The family lived in a big house in the center of town, and the house was open to us teenagers to dance and party on weekends. The mother, a hefty, florid-faced lush, would welcome us in, and let us put all our beer in a side room just off the living room where we partied. She would then help herself to our beer while we were dancing and enjoying ourselves, so she could keep up her liquor supply without spending a cent. My sister and I used to jive together in perfect sync, everyone standing around and watching us. The buzz amongst all the girls was about the older brother who was in the Marines and would come home for periodic visits. All the girls wanted him. He was so good-looking, but shallow and vain, not that we saw that back then. I was one of his boy-crazy followers, and after a night of partying, I accepted a ride home. I had met him a couple times before that night, and seen him driving around with one of the local girls with a bad reputation. One night, after he had dumped her, he came into our driveway and I ran out to meet him. *Oh joy, now it's my turn!* I think we may have driven around for a while with some other people in the car that night; I don't remember the occasion very well.

But back to that fateful party night. By the time I left the party with him, it was around four or five in the morning, and I had been drinking heavily. I don't remember if my sister was at that party or if she had just left earlier or what. Neither do I remember how much the rapist had had to drink, but given his lifestyle and family origins, I'm sure it was a lot. We drove out to a country field in plain view of the highway and started to make out. He demanded sex. I said no. He coerced, said he would never speak to me again. I said no, then relented, then changed my mind to no again. . .the alcohol and exhaustion numbing my reason. My low self-esteem and self-denial as a valuable person led me to care more about whether some no-good bum would ever speak to me again than respecting myself and my right to say no. He insisted, forced himself on me, and half undressed and struggling against his force, I felt the wetness on the outside of my vagina. I had lost my virginity, and he hadn't even penetrated me.

Not only had I thrown a precious pearl to a swine, but luck was against me, and now I was pregnant, all alone with a problem I would have to hide. Maybe it would just go away or maybe I would have a miscarriage, for whom could I confide in that would believe me? I didn't have a boyfriend, hadn't been seen with anyone. Oh the shame of it, that I had accepted that ride home and was now a victim of date rape and sexual assault. . .and what if I had a vene-real disease?

The next day I remember feeling sore from the struggle and thinking, as I looked out the window, *So now I've had sex. What's the big deal?* I didn't feel any different. There had been no pleasure, certainly no orgasm, only shame that I had allowed this. I didn't even recognize it as a rape at that time. After all, I had drunk too much, hadn't I? I had allowed him to take me in his car in the early hours of the morning, so it was my fault, wasn't it?

As I looked out the window that Sunday morning, I saw them driving by, the rapist and his on and off girlfriend. She was looking up and back at the upstairs windows of our house as they drove past, as if he had already told her about the night before. It was a devastating beginning for me regarding issues of trust, love and relationships with the opposite sex. It took many years of therapy to reclaim my own power and birthright, and to learn to respect and love myself enough to demand and even know what I really wanted in a positive and healthy intimate relationship.

I was always the party girl, the jokester looking for fun and laughs, wanting to be accepted, afraid to say no to anyone. Wouldn't I be abused in some way if I said no and expressed how I really felt? So I buried my hurt and pain in looking for fun, adventure and excitement. At that time, I hadn't even thought of my virginity in terms of saving something precious for the one I truly loved. There had been too much misinformation and too many mixed messages and negative images: my mother's promiscuity, my father's denigration of my mother; all those bad experiences mutated into violent energy directed at his daughters, and those adult magazines, with their horrible stories that we found both fascinating and repellent. I remember one story about a violent rape, and how he broke her back as he violated her.

I remember once, as a child of about 6 or 7, I played the role of the Virgin Mary in a Christmas concert play. Wrapped in a white sheet,

I sat in front of the cradle which was holding the "baby Jesus." The sheet was pinned around my arms too tightly for "sleeves," but I was too timid to ask my teacher to adjust the safety pins, so I suffered in silence. A prophetic harbinger of Parthenogenesis? That's what it felt like to me, ten years later, as I asked myself *day after day after day* after that first missed period, *why me? What were the odds of this happening and why is this happening to me? How could this possibly be true?*

Nobody knew what I had done, what had happened to me. In the next few days, my older sister, in her best big-sister condescending voice, asked me quietly how big I thought a man's penis was. It was in the context of a conversation we were having about the mysteries of sex. *If you only knew,* I thought. She never had a clue, and it must have shocked her to the core when she found out the truth.

As time passed and I missed my second period, the quiet horror of the realization that I was definitely pregnant overtook me, and I tried to think of any and every way I could to get out of my predicament. I spent the next few weeks going over and over the same questions in my mind. *Why? Why? What am I going to do? How can this be? What have I done to deserve this? The first time, and not even full penetration!*

Everyone knew of the girls at school who "put out" for their boyfriends. We all knew they'd been screwing around for years. Why didn't *they* get pregnant? Or what about the childless couples who tried for years and years, unable to conceive a child? I felt as if I'd been singled out to suffer by some cruel twist of fate. I tried to think of ways I could abort, but didn't know anything about potions to drink, nor did I know how to research the subject. I used to hit my stomach hard hoping to dislodge the thing, but that never worked, and only made my stomach sore. I slowly started to gain weight, but like many large women, I gained weight everywhere, swelled up like a balloon, so I just looked like I was getting fatter. And nobody knew. I spent a miserable summer living in the fantasy that someone would notice my pregnancy and help me with the problem, or that it would somehow disappear on its own.

By the time school started in September, I had gained quite a lot of weight, but still no one suspected, or at least they never expressed it. They just thought I was "letting myself go." I know that some of my so-called friends ridiculed me behind my back, and I'm sure that some of the townswomen recognized my predicament, but nobody dared say anything. After all, I lived with my father, and some of them probably suspected incest and didn't want to get involved. Who would want to open that Pandora's box? Better to remain silent and feign ignorance.

Whom could I confide in? My so-called mother? Her vicious behavior toward us showed that she didn't really care. How can you treat someone that way, say those mean things, be so hateful and physically and mentally abusive and really love that person? It was as if she wanted to take out all her hate at her miserable and unfulfilled life on her daughters. Why? What did we do to deserve that kind of treatment? She was jealous and competitive, and still is. Miserable, carping, and critical, she will never take responsibility for what she did, which is why she is lonely and desolate in her old age, with all her diseases, one breast, and the penance of living on and on with her memories, her suffering, and her loneliness.

In November of that year, my mother came out from the city to attend a wedding in our town, and she never even guessed that I was eight months pregnant. My schoolwork was abysmal and I felt completely miserable and abandoned, as well as suffering the aches and pains of a normal pregnancy: mood swings, swollen legs and ankles, back pain, and discomfort. How could I possibly concentrate on schoolwork? I was beside myself with worry and fear—fear of being found out, fear of *not* being found out, fear of shaming myself and my family, terrified of going through the experience that awaited me, praying, *Please God, save me from this, please make it go away!* I knew the inevitability of giving birth was fast approaching, but I couldn't face it; I simply could not deal with the reality of having to figure out that whole scenario by myself. I was terrified to tell my father. What if he kicked me out of the house?

Where would I go? I was so exhausted all the time from all the work and all the worry and trying to disguise my growing belly. I tried to ignore it, yet I couldn't; it was driving me crazy. I was frozen in fear and denial. Denial is a reassuring place. It convinces you that the reality doesn't exist, therefore you don't have to deal with it at that moment. Maybe tomorrow something will happen, or there will be a solution, so you keep on going, just trying to get through every day. It saves your sanity by preventing your mind from staring at a truth that you just can't deal with at that moment in time.

I had been so alone for so long with this problem that I went into this locked-in dark place. I was trapped in terror and isolation, with the looming shadow of the inevitable future haunting me. I couldn't find my way out of the forest. I didn't know what to do.

I had always taken an interest in the homely arts, and that Christmas I did find some comfort in baking, cooking, and cleaning the house, not realizing that my maternal nesting instinct was in full bloom. Sometime during those school holidays, my father finally noticed that I was gaining too much weight, even poked my hard stomach and asked me what the problem was. He had a concerned look on his face. I played dumb. Turning away, he said, "After Christmas I'm going to take you to the doctor, because something is wrong here." He must have known—must have at least suspected—but he was probably in denial too. After what happened the following month, I'm sure that conversation must have haunted him.

I went into labor during Math class, at around ten in the morning. The pains started getting stronger and stronger, and it was getting harder and harder to concentrate. If anyone noticed my discomfort, I said that I wasn't feeling well, as I had gone to the bathroom several times that morning feeling nauseous. I managed to walk home for lunch, but I was already in a lot of pain and couldn't wait to get to the solace of my bedroom. It was early January and cold. I don't remember if I ate anything when I got home, or if my father and brother were there. I think I entered the house alone, and went directly to my bedroom without eating, but I'm not sure. I told my father I was feeling sick and couldn't go back to school that afternoon. I stayed in my room all afternoon, lying on my bed under the bedspread, as the pains got sharper.

There was a hockey game that night and we had all planned to go. I think it was a Thursday night, but I'm not sure. My sister had already moved out and was living in a neighboring town, so now I had the bedroom we had always shared completely to myself. There had never been a door to our room at the top of the stairs, and through the haze of my pain I remember my father and brother standing at the doorway to my room, asking if I was all right. They were on their way to the hockey game and were checking in on me. I was close to giving birth I realize now, but I managed to calm my writhing body enough to answer that I was okay. I just wasn't feeling well. I had a stomach ache and just needed to rest.

I heard the car leave the driveway and I remember feeling relief. Now I was finally alone with my problem. I didn't have to keep up the pretense anymore. I was alone and well into labor. I remember thinking, *Maybe I'll die here. That would probably be best.* Then what? Did I pray? Was I too far gone into the pain to think about consequences? Did I ask Jesus to help me?

I don't remember those last moments before giving birth, and as I write this autobiography through an ocean of tears, I know that these words will prime the pump and wrest the memories that have been stuck in my body all these years and that now need to be expressed.

The waves of pain engulfed me. Did I lose consciousness momentarily? I remember removing the clothes from my lower body. There was a gush of water on the bedclothes, and when I thought I would die from the agony and pain contorting and writhing my body, all of a sudden there was a baby there. The pain immediately stopped, and I stared in amazement at a beautiful perfect little baby girl.

A pulsating, electric silence filled the room and there was a resounding, earthy, primordial odor of a new life and a tragic end to both of our innocence—a penance I would carry for the rest of my life.

I couldn't believe my eyes. I don't know what I had expected to see. I think up until that moment, I hadn't thought of it as having a baby inside me; it was just a problem that I had to be rid of. The umbilical cord was still attached to me. The baby was whimpering softly. I panicked and tried to smother her with the pillow, but couldn't do it; I couldn't smother this poor innocent child. Oh dear God, I was so exhausted and there was so much blood. What would my father say when he got home? How was I going to clean all this up before the hockey game was over? I don't remember if I cut the cord before the placenta came out. Did I have some scissors upstairs. . .or a knife? I remember cutting the cord, but did I walk downstairs with the baby attached to me to get something to cut it with? Did I wrap the child in a sheet or towel to carry her while stanching the blood? How could I have managed that? It would have been a lot to carry. I don't have a clear memory of immediately after the birth.

Her crying was getting louder, and I was full of terror, fear, exhaustion, and panic. I had to put the child somewhere so I could clean up everything—hide all the mess. I walked down the stairs to the side door near the bottom step, which led to a landing outside. I wrapped the child in newspaper, which I must have gotten from downstairs when I went for the knife or scissors. I was exhausted, weak, and strangely relieved; it was finally over now. I just had to get rid of all this evidence. I put her outside on that cold January night and went back upstairs to clean up, trying to ignore the sounds of the poor dying child on the other side of the door as I went back and forth up and down the stairs, getting clean sheets, more newspapers, and a pail and water to clean up all the blood stains both in the bedroom and on the floor, the stairs, everywhere. . .

I could hear the child whimpering outside. Why wouldn't she stop and how could I get rid of her? I don't remember the timing clearly, but I know that at some point I must have dressed, put on my boots and outer clothing, and gone outside. I didn't know what I was going to do with her. I just went outside and started walking. I remember cleaning up before and after leaving the house, and I think the crying of my child so upset me that I stopped the clean-up to take her away somewhere so I wouldn't be tortured by the sound of her crying.

The night was cold and crisp with no wind. It hadn't snowed in a few days and the snow crunched hollowly under my feet as I walked through our yard to the main highway. There was no traffic in either direction as I slowly crossed to the other side. I had to get rid of this burden—hide the evidence. Nobody could know. Just dispose of everything and hide it all. It was all my fault. Now I was a murderer on top of everything else I had hidden. Horror just kept building on horror. There was no one to turn to. There would just be more punishment. What could I do? Everything was on my shoulders. I just had to keep on going and figure it out myself.

I was getting cold and losing a lot of blood. Was the child still whimpering? I don't remember. Or had the poor innocent creature died already? I don't think so, even though the umbilical cord was just hanging loose, not tied at all. I had tried to tie it upstairs, but it was too slippery. I was too shaky, and had cut it too short. I reached the neighbor's barn, a few hundred yards from our house. I placed the child in the snow at the side of the barn and left the scene as quickly as possible, anxious to get back to the house and finish cleaning up. I was bleeding profusely, the blood staining the highway as I crossed. I felt very weak, and knew I needed to rest as I was close to fainting. My mind was numb. I was like a robot on automatic pilot going through programmed movements and emotions. None of my actions were thought-out or premeditated. The feelings would come later to haunt me, but that night was basic instinct survival.

I remember gathering up the bloody sheets and pillowcases and putting them in the corner of my closet. The mattress was heavily stained, but I think I covered it with a towel, then put clean sheets back on. There were a lot of bloody newspapers that I had used to stanch the blood, and I remember putting those in the metal garbage can in the corner by the caragana bushes, a few feet from the front storm door. I was getting very tired from all this physical activity. I desperately needed to rest, but I had to keep on going, as they were going to be home soon. Did I remember to clean up the blood from the outside side steps at the foot of the stairs? I couldn't remember. There were just too many things to think about. After I had everything cleaned up, I fell into bed exhausted, and slept. Was I still awake when they came home? I think not, or if I was, I feigned sleep. They probably looked in on me to see if I was okay, and I'm sure everything looked okay from the doorway in the dark. I was using a lot of pads and was afraid I was hemorrhaging. *Maybe I would die now, in my sleep. . .bleed to death, and what a relief it would be from the endless pain and mental torture.*

The next day I stayed home from school and washed clothes. My father had left the house by the time I got up, and my brother was at school. I washed all the bedclothes in the wringer washer and probably any blood stains that were remaining on the floor, stairs, and outside steps. My father came in mid-morning while I was washing clothes and asked how I was feeling. Although I was still quite weak, I was feeling much better physically, and was careful to dress in baggy clothes to hide the fact that my stomach bump was gone. I was still bleeding heavily but less than the night before, and even though I was going through a lot of pads, I knew I wasn't hemorrhaging.

The guilt, remorse, and sheer enormity of what I had done started to sink in. The whole thing was so surreal. Now that the evidence was gone, the three of us sitting at the table eating dinner, outwardly seemed so normal, yet inwardly I was consumed with terrible remorse and regret. Had all that really happened last night, or was it just a bad dream? I had little appetite, did the dishes, and escaped to my room so my face and actions wouldn't reveal my worry and tormented thoughts.

I went back to school the next day, and as the days wore on, I became severely depressed and was quietly going out of my mind about what I had done. I thought I was going to go crazy with the vivid memories of that night. I couldn't concentrate. I was withdrawn, and thoughts of what I'd done consumed me. How could I go on? When I walked home from school, I couldn't bear to look over at the barn where my poor innocent daughter lay dead. Maybe I should just kill myself too. But how would I do it? How could I have done what I did? How I wanted to hold her close to me, but it was too late. *How can I live with this? I can't stand these thoughts!*

What would become of me? How could I possibly say anything now, after all that had transpired? How could I even broach the subject? Who would believe the horror?

I was lactating profusely. I had to stuff cloths inside my bra so the milk stains wouldn't show. Every time I thought about my abandoned daughter, the lactating seemed to get worse. *Please God. . .please. . .please help me with this. . .*

I prayed and prayed in those days, trying to control my thoughts and preserve my sanity as my guilt and sorrow haunted me. I prayed for deliverance, for help, and ten days after the birth, merciful help did come in the form of a chinook wind.

For those not familiar with the term, a chinook is a warm, dry wind which sometimes occurs during the winter months, producing a sudden rise in temperature, resulting in unusually mild, spring-like weather. This phenomenon is common farther west in the foothills, but not in our area; it was an unusual occurrence which proved to be a godsend. There was a sudden thaw. It was a Sunday, and everyone was outside enjoying the unseasonably warm January weather.

It was mid-afternoon in bright sunlight and the trees were dripping with melting ice and snow. I had an uneasy sense of foreboding. All of a sudden there was a knock at the door, and I opened it to see a pale and extremely distraught man standing there, shaking. With a trembling voice, he asked to speak to my father. I didn't know him very well, but knew he lived in town with his wife and young children. I called my father to the door, heartsick, for I knew by the queasy, nauseous feeling in my stomach exactly what he was there for. I stayed close in the background, and heard him tell my father to come quickly with him to the neighbor's barn. His children had been playing there and had found a baby.

My father accompanied him to the grave site, then quickly came back to the house to call the police. He told me that the children had found a baby lying there. "Just lying there in the melting snow," he said, "with her arms folded like a little doll." How he must have suffered later when he realized he had been looking at his first grandchild.

I expressed shock and horror, letting out some of my emotion, but I was terrified and felt sick to my stomach. I didn't say much, because I thought I was going to throw up. The local police arrived quickly and talked briefly to my father and to me, asking us if we'd heard or seen anything recently in the area—had we seen anyone pregnant, or anyone likely to have abandoned a child. My father said no and I denied any involvement. Later that day the serious crimes unit came down from the city and swarmed all over the scene. My father looked out the window. "Once the big boys from the city start investigating," he said, "it won't take them long to find out who did this." I just put my head down.

The flurry of activity continued near our house, just across from the driveway by the neighbor's barn. Our neighbors were middle-aged bachelors, so I knew the police would be coming back to our house, as it was the closest house with a female resident. I stayed quietly indoors. When they finally knocked on our door later that afternoon, they asked my father if they could come in and ask us a few more questions about the sequence of events of that day. Had we seen anything or anyone unusual recently? Did we know any details about any recent uncommon events in the area? They were watching me closely, but I wasn't admitting anything. I still felt that I had to keep it all inside. It had been there for so long, how could I possibly say anything now? I had terrors of being hauled off to jail, being locked up forever, and of everyone judging me for the monster that I was, after having done what I did.

We had stew that night for dinner and I could barely eat, but I had to keep up the pretense of normalcy. I knew in my heart that this was the end of the road for me—that from now on it was just a matter of time. My secret would be out, the horror would be revealed, and deep down I felt relief, as I had never known such mental torture and hell as I had experienced in the last ten days. I'll never forget that last meal at home before I was arrested, and I've never eaten stew since that night.

That evening, around 7:30, the local police returned to the house for a second interrogation. I was familiar with these police officers, as my sister was engaged to one of them from the same law enforcement office in the neighboring town where she worked, however her fiance was not present at the interrogation. They were nice to me, calm and relaxed. There was no pressure; they were just quietly asking me questions.

I was evasive and uncomfortable, not admitting anything, until finally one of the officers said to me, "We know you know something about this," and pointed to my sweatshirt, which was stained with long streaks down the front. And during the thaw, they said they had found blood stains in the snow, on the ground between our garbage can and the front steps, as well as some bloody newspapers in the garbage can.

I could no longer take the pressure and started to cry. Covering my face with my hands, and sobbing uncontrollably, I blurted out my confession between sobs: "I'm a murderer. . .I'm a murderer. . .I'm a murderer. . ."

My father, my big macho, unemotional father, was hunched over in his usual chair at the end of the kitchen table, his massive shoulders rigid, his head bowed way down low. I think he must have been crying. As I write these words, now about the age my father was at that time, with grown children of my own, I realize how horrible it must have been for him to hear of such a tragedy happening to his own child and grandchild, and how responsible and guilty he must have felt.

When I started to write this book, I was afraid that I would release uncontrollable emotions and be unable to handle all the memories brought to the forefront. But what came up for me was all the sorrow and pain my family had felt at the time—all the emotion and stress that those around me had suffered—and how my family, who loved me, had to cope in the days following my arrest. How much of a shock it must have been for them to hear of such a sad and tragic incident that had gone unnoticed, happening right under their noses, and the guilt and remorse they must have felt knowing that I had suffered all those months, all on my own. They had been there with me all the time and hadn't known; they hadn't been able to help me. It wasn't just me who suffered terribly. They had too.

As I write this so many years later, I still grieve for my daughter and for the lost future of our youth, hers and mine. I also grieve for the suffering of my family, my relatives and my loved ones. The shock and anguish they must have felt at hearing the news.

Months later, after I was back home, one of the local women said to me, "Your father sure went to bat for you." We never, ever spoke about this while he was alive, but I'm grateful and appreciative that my father, and all my family, did stand by me and support me in such a loving way.

CHAPTER 6

The Aftermath

ONCE I HAD ADMITTED WHAT I HAD DONE, THE officer quietly read me my rights. He cautioned me that I didn't have to say anything without the presence of a lawyer, and that anything I said from then on could be used in a court of law against me. But I was too emotionally far gone to stop. All the horror had been held inside of me for too long, and I kept sobbing out my feelings, repeating over and over that I was a murderer and a horrible person after what I had done. My father remained silent and speechless, trying to get control of his emotions.

The officer quietly advised my father that it would be a good idea to retain legal counsel, and then told me that I was under arrest and would probably require medical attention. They explained that now I was in police custody and they would be taking me to the hospital in the neighboring town. We had a hospital in our town, so I don't know why they didn't take me there. Maybe it was the choice of the police, or maybe they had asked my father his preference of location for medical attention for me.

They asked my father which of the three doctors in the neighboring town he wanted to care for me, then told me to put on my coat and boots. We were leaving immediately. It was around eight or nine at night. I don't remember if my father said anything to me, or even if my little brother was present through all of this. Had he gone to bed? I think so, as I don't remember him being present during the questioning or even in the next room. I do remember leaving the house in the cold and wind and getting in the back of the police cruiser, with my father sitting beside me. If my brother was asleep in bed, who stayed behind and looked after him? I don't know and can't remember any discussion around that. They didn't put me in handcuffs, and as I sat quietly looking through the darkened windows, the whole scene felt surreal. I had never been in a police car before. The panels and lights on the dashboard glowed red and white, the crackling of the police radio interrupting the small talk between my father and the officers—under the circumstances you couldn't really call it a conversation. "Well, this is the first time I've ever been in a police cruiser," my father said, laughing nervously.

We arrived at the hospital and I was taken to an examination room by the nuns who ran the hospital. The doctor was there, and he gently examined me and then spoke quietly to my father. . .was he in the room with me? I can't remember, but I don't think so. At any rate, he told him that I had a severe tear, and that I would have to have an operation later to repair that. I don't know why they didn't do it then, when the scar tissue was fresh. Maybe because of the dictates of the police, for now I was under arrest and in their custody. The nuns put me in a private room and gave me pills to dry up the breast milk, as well as a tranquilizer, as I was very distraught. I was glad to be in a place of solitude. Now I could finally rest and be taken care of.

My father and sister came to see me the next day, and told me that I would continue to receive medication to keep me calm and relaxed. After my hospital stay, my father explained that I would be sent to a psychiatric facility for a thirty-day observation, to see if I was fit to stand trial. He told me that he thought this was a good idea—for me to be examined by a psychiatrist—apart from it being ordered by the police. He also told me that my child had been examined and that she would have died anyway due to respiratory problems. I didn't believe him then, and to this day I don't believe it. I think he was just trying his best to make me feel better.

The next day our local minister came to see me and was asking me some questions about the birth: how had I cut the cord, what did I do with the placenta, etc. These questions were upsetting to me, but I didn't know how not to answer them. At his suggestion, we prayed. Later that same day, a girl from my hometown stopped by my room, as she was also in the hospital. It was none other than the rapist's sometime girlfriend, asking me questions, wanting to know if I had heard about what had happened in our town—slyly trying to glean information as she casually looked out the window. In both these situations, it was very stressful to be interrogated and reminded of that night, and of having to avoid the truth.

When my sister came to see me that night, she was furious that those people had so disrespectfully entered my room to question me. She demanded that the nuns put a quarantine on my room and not allow anyone entry except immediate family members and the police, if necessary. She brought me a new nightgown and housecoat that day, as I had left the house with nothing but the clothes on my back.

I heard some rumors while I was there. When I was feeling well enough to leave my room and walk in the corridor, passing the sitting room, I could hear some of the other patients discussing the news: "We heard that that young girl's parents kicked her out of the house, and that's why she abandoned her baby. Now they'll really be in trouble. . ."

A few days later, I was discharged from the hospital and was released into police custody. I was immediately taken to the local courthouse, where I was read the charges the police had filed against me.

I was charged with non-capital murder, manslaughter, infanticide, and concealment. The judge asked me if I understood the charges of the Crown against me, and I said yes. He then ordered the thirty-day psychiatric assessment to be done at a large mental hospital in a city several hours to the south of us.

I don't remember if my father was present at that hearing. I don't think so. As we left the courthouse, the police officers explained that we would be leaving for the mental hospital the next day. They were very kind to me. They spoke quietly and respectfully, and carefully explained that as I was under arrest I would have to spend that night in jail. They said the local jail was full, so they would be taking me to a neighboring town, which was much smaller and quieter and had an empty jail at that moment. In retrospect, I think the real reason they didn't incarcerate me in that town was that they didn't want to place me with all the local drunks, some of whom might have known me or my family, or who may have known the family name. There were lots of rumors swirling around, and they didn't want to subject me to all the gossip.

We left the courthouse and drove to the neighboring town. I felt very alone, and even more so when we drove up to the jail. The officer's wife let me into the small cell, apologizing for having to bolt the door behind me. I said that I understood. We were both nervous and I'm sure the situation was as unfamiliar to her as it was to me; she had probably never had to lock up an attractive, polite young woman in a cell before. She brought me a tray of supper, and I spent a restless night on the hard cot, covered with a rough, gray army blanket, watching a TV through the bars. We never had a TV at home, and I wasn't much interested in it. I hardly slept, wondering what kind of experiences awaited me in the mental hospital. I got up early, washed up at the sink, then picked at my breakfast tray with little appetite. I was relieved to see the sergeant who had arrived to take me to the hospital and I was glad to be leaving that gray, depressing place. I couldn't help but wonder if that was where I would eventually end up for a very long time, once my case came to trial.

The sergeant, accompanied by his wife, drove me to the mental hospital, about a four-hour drive from the jail. They admitted me to the psychiatric ward, and as I was still under arrest and in police custody, I was assigned a nurse for every shift, who had to accompany me wherever I went, twenty-four hours a day. My first glimpse of that ward horrified me, and looking around, I felt afraid of all these very strange people I would be living with for the next thirty days. The sergeant's wife saw my disconcerted expression, leaned over, and whispered, "You're not like them." It made me feel better and I always appreciated her saying that to me. Years later, when I saw the Jack Nicholson movie, *One Flew Over the Cuckoo's Nest*, the psychiatric patients in the movie reminded me of those many interesting characters that I met on that psych ward.

The sergeant and his wife wished me well and left, and there I was, all alone in lunatic land. My first assigned nurse was a woman of about thirty, who immediately asked me how I had managed. What could I say? By then I was sick and tired of all the dumb questions directed at me, but of course that was just the beginning. There were endless questions and analyses still to come.

What followed was a month of physical discomfort, loneliness, and me facing my demons. I was very anemic, and so was prescribed iron pills, which made me very constipated. The food was starchy and processed—typical hospital fare. I was used to walking a lot at home, and in the hospital I wasn't getting my usual exercise; generally I felt very unhappy and very uncomfortable. Some of my assigned nurses asked me questions about my ordeal. Most didn't, but were always open to me sharing if I wanted to, and I usually didn't want to.

I was assigned a disinterested Filipino psychiatrist whom I saw once a week. He asked me a lot of questions and acted very bored during our sessions together, looking everywhere but at me— examining his fingernails or looking skyward. I didn't enjoy those visits, and didn't feel I benefited anything from them. My mother later commented that his disinterested attitude was intentional, to see if I was "on the ball."

The only medication I was taking were the iron pills, but I did have to go for two EEGs and an ECG. The EEGs were awful, as they had to glue wires to my scalp to record the brainwaves and afterwards my hair was sticky with the glue, and tore my hair out when I tried to remove it. It reminded me of the good old days when my mother used to live on the farm.

I learned to view the patients from a philosophical viewpoint, and even came to enjoy my interaction with some of them. Psychiatric patients can be the most interesting, intelligent, perceptive people, and often very amusing. They are highly sensitive, which is one of the reasons they're all nuts. There were a few younger patients there, and sometimes we would stay up late in the rec room, listening to old Dean Martin and Frank Sinatra records, my constant nurse trailing me wherever I went. Many were there for depression or "nervous breakdowns," and they would always ask me why I was there. To them I seemed all right, and I didn't have a long list of meds to take, as most of them did. They would ask me if I was having shock treatments, and tell me how horrible it was. I saw some patients come back from their shock treatments looking like zombies, and I thank God that was not my fate. I always made up some excuse for being there; I was good at hiding and evading the truth. I had learned that lies of omission were the best defense, otherwise I was exposed to too many questions.

I had visitors while I was in the psych ward; my father, brother, and sister came to see me several times. My family was in good spirits, and we were all happy to see each other. I could tell they were relieved to see that I was looking and feeling much better, maybe not so much physically because of the food and lack of exercise, but certainly mentally. They never asked me about any details of that night, but my father did comment, "The Good Lord was with you that night, my dear." I also overheard him say to my aunt, sometime later, that I was "as strong as an ox," to have survived such an ordeal.

When I complained about the food or my physical discomfort during those visits, my father especially encouraged me, telling me that it was good for me to be there in the hospital—that it was a beneficial experience for me, that it was just for a short time, and that I should be positive and look to the future. My father told me that he had retained a lawyer from the same firm that had handled the marriage separation and custody of us children. The senior partner's son was an up-and-coming criminal lawyer and he did a great job. But more about that later.

I became friends with some of my constant chaperones, and toward the end of my stay, one of the nurses invited me to her home for lunch. I was so excited to be going on a day trip out of the institution. This was allowed, as I had been a model patient, and she was a registered psychiatric nurse and so fulfilled the role of police chaperone. We drove to her apartment, which I remember was on the upstairs floor of a house. As we drove, I looked around at the bustle of city activity, appreciating so much the freedom and variety of viewing everyday city life after having been locked up so long.

She made us lunch, and I don't remember what we ate, but for dessert she had made homemade marshmallows. I had never heard of homemade marshmallows before. They tasted the same as the commercial ones, only fresher and made in a rectangular pan, cut into squares. I asked her for the recipe and I still have it, written out in her handwriting. Never made it, but still have it. Gelatin, cream of tartar, white sugar, egg white.

I also had friends come to visit me from my mother's city—friends that I had come to know during our regular visits there. One friend had just gotten married, as we were now into February, so she and her new husband came, as well as her older sister. It was nice to see them and I appreciated the visit, but things were very different now, for them and for me.

My mother also came down to visit me. I had not spoken to her or heard from her since November. I don't remember if she wrote and told me she was coming or if she just showed up. I remember she was quick to tell me that she had "lost her job" due to the publicity, but it was probably she who had left her employment, embarrassed at having to listen to the gossip, full of guilt and shame at her neglect as a mother. She never once asked me about the details of that night or empathized or commented on the events; however she was full of criticism and condemnation for my father and the townspeople for not having noticed my condition. She said they were all "guilty as hell." Never mind that she had seen me when I was eight months pregnant, after not having seen me for a year prior to that, and *she* never had a clue. As I've said, denial is a reassuring place, and she has always been a master at relegating blame and responsibility to others, rather than taking a good look at herself. As my father commented some time later, "If she had been home here where she belonged, this wouldn't have happened."

During that one visit, my mother made a point of telling me all the dirt and scandal of all the townspeople, how this one had had an illegitimate baby, how that one had committed a terrible crime or brought dishonor to the family. I don't remember it all, nor was I all that interested in what others had done; I had enough of my own problems to deal with. But I understood why she was telling me. What she was trying to say was that others had experienced tragedy, delinquency, and sorrow and had lived through their ordeal and overcome it. "It's nothing to be ashamed of or proud of," she said. "It's just something that happened."

I also received many beautiful cards and letters from the people in my town, which I very much appreciated and still have. They assured me that I was in their thoughts and prayers, and I really felt that warmth and love directed toward me. It made the thought of returning to my community easier to bear.

As the date approached for the time of my release from the hospital, I remember thinking, *Now I really have to face the music.* I would have to return to school, walk the streets of our small town, and face all the townspeople, my classmates, and everybody from the entire community. I don't remember the trip back home, but the police must have picked me up, because before I could return home I had to be released from police custody. The first stop was the courthouse, where bail was set for $10,000. My father put his farm up as collateral, and I was free to go back and live with my family until the court case.

I don't recall at what stage in all this drama I was asked who the father of the child was. I think it was early on, while I was still in the hospital, and I told the truth. My father later asked me why I had done that with someone I hardly knew. I didn't tell him the truth about the rape. In fact, I didn't even identify it as such until years later. I just said I was curious. After I was home from the mental hospital, he said that on the advice of my lawyer, they had decided not to prosecute him or go after him in any way as there was no point. The male perspective—let the woman go down alone and carry the brunt of the pain and the shame. I'm sure much of that decision was to avoid further scandal in the town, as the rapist had left town, never to return. Just forget about it and let it blow over. If I had had a caring mother there to support me, he would have had to assume some responsibility, at the very least financial.

I'm sure there were some who thought it might even have been a case of incest, as I lived with my father. Even my mother voiced this suspicion, but of course she *would* have those thoughts, now wouldn't she?

Small town country life is so accommodating. Life goes back to its usual routine, the stoic farm people accepting life's fate, adjusting to the inevitability and acknowledgment of the tragedy, grateful that I was alive and well, that everything was back to normal, and that the media attention had died down. Life just goes on like the predictability of the seasons. Back to school?

Yes, after the horror, I went back to school. I steeled myself for that first day of attendance, but everyone was so nice to me, welcoming me with smiles and genuine caring. Some asked me how I was feeling, and they all tried to show me that they were glad to see me back home, that I was still welcome and loved there despite what I had done.

Nobody talked about what I had done or referred to it in any way. I never had any counseling and everyone just tried to forget it ever happened. I should have left—gone to live with one of my aunts on the West coast and finished high school there—but my father had enough expenses to think about what with the lawyer's fees. He'd had to put up his farm for collateral as bail for my release into the community, hadn't he? And who would have looked after my little brother and tended to all the housework? After all, as my father said at the trial, I was "handy to have around the house."

I wasn't the first girl in the community to have an illegitimate child, but those other girls had gone away and lived with relatives in other cities for a year or so, then we gradually heard about it later. My situation was by far worse than any of theirs, yet I just came back home and continued the school year.

Of course everything had changed for me, and I couldn't wait to leave that small town and my former life behind. One of the older male nurses had given me some good advice before I left the mental hospital. "You've got your whole life ahead of you," he said. "You're losing weight and you have a beautiful face. You could be a model. Forget about the past, and don't be afraid to move forward—you're only 18 years old."

I had lost a lot of weight, and was proud and happy with the way I looked, trying on clothes that had been too tight for me, and admiring myself in the mirror. When my father saw me doing this, he had only disparaging remarks for me. "Don't get into that too much," he said, always afraid of "the difficulties" his daughters' beauty might lead to, but what could it possibility have led to that was worse than what I had already done? It was so much simpler for everyone, myself included, for me to eat lots and stay fat—it was so safe, and such an avoidance of men and dating. Even some of the townspeople commented at my trimness, saying, "You look like you need a good meal."

I was never encouraged to celebrate and honor my beauty and look my best; I was just supposed to make everyone feel comfortable by escaping behind the fat. It took me years to learn to value and love myself. My sister told me some years later that after I came home from the hospital our father had expressed to her that the best thing would be for me to get married as soon as possible. I was too smart for that fate, and had learned from my mistake.

I finished grade eleven that year, but had no interest in participating in any of the school activities that I used to long to attend. The year-end school prom came and went, and many asked me why I hadn't attended. I was a woman now and couldn't wait to leave that small town and start a new life in the city. I was planning a career in psychiatric nursing, and my thoughts were now far beyond the parameters of a pastoral country existence.

I ended up staying another year and completing my grade twelve, but it was only a partial and my heart wasn't in it, as I just wanted to be gone from that town and all those memories. I did complete the remainder of my studies years later, before I obtained my university degrees.

In those first few months back home, I was looking forward to a new independent future, but those thoughts were always tempered by the uncertainty of my impending trial, which had been set for the fall of that year. Would I go to jail? Would I be separated from my family and familiar surroundings, and sent to the federal penitentiary for women in the East? The maximum penalty for the charges against me was twenty-five years to life.

During the summer holidays of that year, after many reminders to my father, I went back to the hospital to have the tear in my perineum repaired. I don't know that it did much good, as it should have been done when I was first hospitalized. During my recovery on the gynecology ward, there were many curious questions from the other women as to why I was there. Again, I avoided detail. I just gave them vague answers; furthermore, I didn't owe them any explanations.

I slowly started to go out with my friends again, but had to be careful about what I did, as I was out on bail and had to comply with certain conditions. I remember once being in a car that was stopped by the police; we had liquor in the back and I was underage. I felt the fear of exposure, but the police officer said nothing at the time. Several days later, my sister had a talk with me, reminding me of my precarious position, and to lay low until the trial was over.

I started grade twelve in the fall, with my trial looming ever closer on the horizon. I had started to see my lawyer occasionally, and admired him for his sophistication and elán. He must have been in his late thirties or early forties, and seemed to me to be highly intelligent and worldly. Several weeks before the trial, we had to go to court to choose the twelve-person jury. He had coached me carefully on what was about to happen. As each person was called up as a possible juror, I was to look them straight in the eye.

"Don't look away under any circumstances," he said. I don't remember how many people I had to stare down that day, but they were mostly men. It took a lot of courage to gaze unswervingly at all those pairs of eyes, some of them judgmental, already condemning. I remember one in particular: a middle-aged man who had taught at our high school. He had taught my sister in the higher grades and all the students had made fun of him and complained about what a disaster of a teacher he was. He glared at me for a long time, his eyes bulging out, red and watery. I didn't look away from that intense gaze and my own eyes must have been as fearsome as his. He wasn't chosen as one of the jurors, and I went home exhausted that day, even more worried about the upcoming trial, as the raw emotion of that day had brought all the memories back in sharp focus, and I knew I would relive them again even more vividly at the trial.

Immediately before the trial, my lawyer again coached me on my behavior during the court proceedings and the showing of evidence at the trial. "Don't show any emotion," he said. "No screaming, no crying, no dramatics. . .just sit there quietly." He even told me what to wear. "Make sure it's something simple, modest, and conservative. Preferably a dark color." I wore a sleeveless, dark green sheath dress that I had made myself.

The big day finally arrived in early October—a beautiful sunny, crisp fall day. My trial was held in the neighboring town, as there was no courthouse in our village and the law states that the trial must be held as close as possible to the community where the crime was committed. It also happened to be a pro day, when all the high school students were out of class. What luck for me. The trial lasted five days and the courtroom was packed every day. The jurors were eleven men and one woman. Of course the locals were curious to hear all the details. I looked straight ahead as I entered the courtroom, not looking to my right where everyone was seated, nor at the jurors seated to my left, nor even using my peripheral vision. I became more and more exhausted as the days wore on and was hardly sleeping at night, but I kept my composure through it all.

I remember there were recesses and lunch breaks, but we never left the courthouse. Did someone bring lunch in? I don't remember, but they must have. On that first day, during the first recess, one of the local high school students whom I knew from social and sports events, brought me an orange pop. He was the one who told me that it was a pro day, but that—in support of me—the students had decided not to attend. He said they were all thinking of me and wished me the very best. I appreciated that and was so touched by his words. I'll always remember that kind gesture and those caring thoughts.

At the end of the week-long trial, the jury deliberated for several hours and finally delivered a not-guilty verdict. I had been acquitted of all four charges.

My father later told me that it was the one woman on the jury who had saved me from a criminal record. She had insisted that I was innocent, and convinced the others to her way of thinking, explaining to them a woman's unstable mental state after giving birth. He also told me that the judge had informed my lawyer, even before the trial started, that whatever the outcome of the jurors' decision, he wouldn't send me to jail—that in the event of a conviction he would hand down a suspended sentence.

I walked out of that courtroom a free woman, and even though the general public had already left, there were a few well-wishers. One of the police officers approached me and quietly told me to try and just forget about everything that had happened and to get on with my life. I had my whole life ahead of me; I should just put this whole incident behind me. My lawyer's parting advice was to tell me that one day, when I married, I would have to tell my life partner about what I had done. I have mixed feelings when I say that I never had to make that disclosure.

By the end of the trial I was completely drained and exhausted, and I felt relieved that it was finally over and I could go forward with my life. I had hope for the future; if only it were that easy to forget about those terrifying moments in my bedroom, the aftermath, the guilt and remorse. . .how it would forever haunt me and shape me, particularly as I matured.

EPILOGUE

NO ONE IN MY IMMEDIATE FAMILY HAS EVER MEN-
tioned this incident in all these years. When I was in my late twenties, my aunt tried to broach the subject and asked me why I hadn't
confided in anyone about my pregnancy. I remained silent and did
not respond in any way, because words lead to questions and questions lead to explanations, rationalizations and justifications, and
there is never an end or a solution. What's done is done; there is
no going back and no point in discussing it. My aunt didn't press
me for information, but I know she would have been interested in
reading this book.

When I reflect on the trajectory of my life, I can see that had I
not experienced what I did and committed such a crime, my life
would have been completely different, yet I can't even imagine
what that alternative life might have looked like.

That long-ago incident was my destiny, an unusual circumstance
and survival that led me down a different life path, and I feel
blessed for all that I have experienced in my lifetime. I feel especially honored that I had the opportunity to become a mother
again, as well as a godmother.

My life has not been easy, nor has it been the most difficult; there are those who have suffered much more than I have, and I am grateful and count my blessings every day.

Several years ago I read about a woman who had been raped; it was her first sexual experience and she became pregnant. A devout Catholic, her religion forbade her to have an abortion, so she had the child. She was blonde. Her assailant was a black man, and her son looked just like him. She said that every time she looked at her child it reminded her of the rape. I remember thinking, *Which situation is more difficult to bear, hers or mine?*

If you are reading this book and have experienced similar trauma in your life, I hope that you can stay strong and find the healing spiritual path to finally forgive yourself and move on.

It has been a long road to recovery and healing for me, and there is one thing I have learned and am absolutely sure of: We all have a choice of how we react to life's dark and inexplicable passages. We can buckle under the burden of them or we can hold our heads high and become fearless. I chose the latter.

"Adversity introduces a man to himself"

- Albert Einstein

CPSIA information can be obtained
at www.ICGtesting.com
Printed in the USA
LVOW07*0331150817
544990LV00005B/30/P